OFF THE BEATEN TRACK

Volume II: Pisgah

Jim Parham

WMC
Publishing

Also by Jim Parham:

OFF THE BEATEN TRACK
Volume I: A Guide to Mountain Biking
in Western North Carolina—
The Smokies

OFF THE BEATEN TRACK
Volume III: A Guide to Mountain Biking
in North Georgia

OFF THE BEATEN TRACK
Volume IV: A Guide to Mountain Biking
in East Tennessee

49 Fun & Inexpensive Things
To Do In The Smokies
With Children

WMC Publishing, P.O. Box 158, Almond, NC 28702

ISBN 0-9631861-6-7 $12.95
ISSN 1076-6189

Cover design by Ron Roman

A great deal of information is contained in this book, and every effort has been
made to provide this information as accurately as possible. Roads and trails,
however, can change with time; some roads and trails may not be marked by signs;
distances may vary with individual cyclocomputers; and land agency rules and
regulations are subject to interpretation and change. There are risks inherent in
the sport of mountain biking. *The author and publisher accept no responsibility*
for inaccuracies or for damages incurred while attempting any of the routes
listed.

Printed in the United States on recycled paper.

Volume II:

A Guide to Mountain Biking in Western North Carolina

Pisgah

Jim Parham

TABLE OF CONTENTS

THE TRAILS

INTRODUCTION

In 1992 when I wrote the first edition of this book, I felt like I had discovered a world-class mountain biking destination. Now, after spending years riding all over the country, I am certain of it.

The Pisgah District of the Pisgah National Forest in western North Carolina is a 157,000-square-mile chunk of land on either side of the Blue Ridge Parkway just west of Asheville, North Carolina. Most folks just call it Pisgah. This is a very unique place, with hundreds of miles of designated bike trails that are well marked and well maintained, mountains that rise to over 6,000 feet, waterfalls springing from most every stream, enormous rock outcroppings erupting from the dense forest—all this and more in an undeveloped, wild area that is easy to get to. You can find trails that will have you swooshing through dark, green tunnels of mountain laurel and rhododendron, and others where you'll splash through streams and wade whitewater rivers. You can ride to the ridge tops and around sheer rock faces and then zoom back down again after seeing some stunning views. You'll find backcountry camping, public campgrounds, picnic areas, trailhead parking lots, bike shops and lodging nearby, and good roads to take you from one ride to the next.

It seems that mountain cyclists are now discovering what other recreationists found out decades ago: Pisgah is a great place to be any time of the year. In summer, the mountains are cool, green and lush. Afternoon thunderstorms are not uncommon. At this time of year you can expect to see fishermen and people floating in inner tubes in the streams. You might see youth groups or families hiking and camping in the backcountry. Some of the trails are designated for horse use as well, and you might encounter equestrians, especially in the South Mills and Avery Creek areas. It is also not too uncommon to see climbers on the towering cliffs, and meet llama packers and covered wagons.

Fall is known as leaf season, and it attracts a different crowd. Look for slow driving cars on the forest roads as passengers crane their necks to see splashes of red, yellow and orange on the trees. Fall and early winter are also hunting season. You'll want to take caution and wear bright colored clothing, such as blaze orange, at this time of year.

Winter, of course, brings colder temperatures and another well kept secret: Pisgah is a great place to ride in the winter. It doesn't snow too often, especially at the lower elevations. There are no leaves on the trees, so the views are spectacular and unobstructed, and it's not uncommon to have sunny 60° days in December, January and February. It might also be cold and rainy, so watch the weather patterns closely before heading into the hills. Fewer people frequent the area at this time so a number of seasonal use trails become available to bikers.

Spring starts sometime in March and goes into May. With it comes new, bright green leaves, thousands of varieties of wildflowers, and people of all types ready to hit the trails. Keeping in mind that Pisgah is a multi-use forest, you can also expect to see timber harvesting, log trucks and maintenance crews any time of the year.

As you ride in Pisgah, you may wonder how the trails stay in such good condition. Many thanks go to the Asheville area Blue Ridge Bike Club and the Pisgah District's rangers and staff. These folks have done everything right to ensure that trails remain open to mountain bike use. Every month, members of the bike club can be seen out repairing and maintaining sections of trail. District officials monitor the trails and provide work crews as well. Pisgah could serve well as a model for other trails access groups across the country.

This book lists the best rides in Pisgah. Whether you are a first-time rider or an expert, you'll find rides to suit your tastes and abilities. Study the "How To Use This Book" section on the following pages and choosing the best routes will come easier. Also keep in mind that the Pisgah area is very rugged. Some people find even the easier trails to be difficult.

I hope you will have the time, as I have, to give all of these rides a try so that you can see for yourself what a wonderful place Pisgah is to ride a bike.

J.P.
June, 1995

How To Use This Book

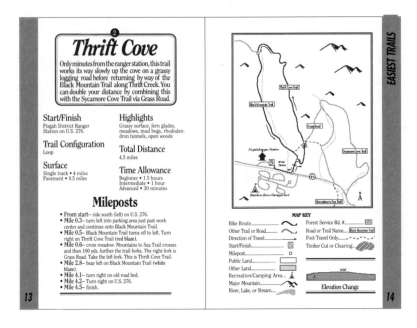

② Thrift Cove

Only minutes from the ranger station, this trail works its way slowly up the cove on a grassy logging road before returning by way of the Black Mountain Trail along Thrift Creek. You can double your distance by combining this with the Sycamore Cove Trail via Grass Road.

Start/Finish
Pisgah District Ranger Station on U.S. 276.

Trail Configuration
Loop

Surface
Single track • 4 miles
Pavement • 0.5 miles

Highlights
Grassy surface, fern glades, meadows, mud bogs, rhododendron tunnels, open woods

Total Distance
4.5 miles

Time Allowance
Beginner • 1.5 hours
Intermediate • 1 hour
Advanced • 30 minutes

Mileposts

- From start– ride south (left) on U.S. 276.
- Mile 0.3– turn left into parking area just past work center and continue onto Black Mountain Trail.
- Mile 0.5– Black Mountain Trail turns off to left. Turn right on Thrift Cove Trail (red blaze).
- Mile 0.6– cross meadow. Mountains to Sea Trail crosses and then 100 yds. further the trail forks. The right fork is Grass Road. Take the left fork. This is Thrift Cove Trail.
- Mile 2.8– bear left on Black Mountain Trail (white blaze).
- Mile 4.1– turn right on old road bed.
- Mile 4.2– Turn right on U.S. 276.
- Mile 4.5– finish.

MAP KEY

Bike Route
Other Trail or Road
Direction of Travel
Start/Finish
Milepost
Public Land
Other Land
Recreation/Camping Area
Major Mountain
River, Lake, or Stream

Forest Service Rd. #
Road or Trail Name
Foot Travel Only
Timber Cut or Clearing

Elevation Change

Typical Route Description Pages

- The **route number** appears in either a circle, a square or a diamond at the top of the left-hand page. The number corresponds to the route number in the table of contents, and the circle (easiest), square (more difficult) or diamond (most difficult) indicates the route difficulty.

- **Route difficulty** (also shown vertically at the top right-hand corner of the right page) is relative to this book and the Pisgah District. Due to the extreme topography, you'll find all these routes to be somewhat more difficult than those in other parts of the Southeast. You will also find the ratings I've given these routes may be different from the original Forest Service hiker trail ratings that appear on the signs.

- Below the **route name** is a brief description of the route's more noted highlights.

- **Start/Finish** indicates where the route begins and how to get there.

- **Trail Configuration** describes the type of route.

- There are three **Surface** types: single track, forest road and pavement. This will show how many miles of each surface to expect.

- In the **Highlights** there will be a one or two-word description of things you can expect on the trail. For example: *Horse use* means you may encounter horses, that the trail will have rutted areas with loose rocks, and that any wet places can be very muddy.

- **Total Distance** shows the number of miles you will travel.

- **Time Allowance** is a rough approximation of the time it will take you to ride the trail with *minimal* stops, according to your ability level.

- Each **milepost** corresponds to the adjoining map. The first milepost is at the Start/Finish and is represented by an Ⓢ on the map. There is a milepost for every turn or any other place of note, and each is represented by a ☐ on the map.

- The **maps** are oriented north, with all roads or trails marked by name or number. All roads, trails, buildings, clearings and other features relevant to the route are shown, as well as the best direction of travel. Some of the routes listed in this book can be linked together for shorter or longer rides. When this is the case, those trails or roads are also shown on the map; however, no mileposts or directions are given for these. **Maps are not drawn to scale**.

- The **Map Key** shows what each symbol represents, as well as indicating the shading used for different types of trails, roads or land. The main route is always shown in black.

- By looking at the **Elevation Change**, you can get a pretty good idea where the major hills are on the route, how long they will be, and the degree of steepness. It does not show every short rise or dip in the trail.

Other Sections

- There are two sections immediately following this page that cover **Mountain Bike Etiquette** and **Riding In The Pisgah National Forest**. Knowing and following the rules and using good judgement are critical in keeping public land available to mountain bikers.

- On the **Orientation Pages** you'll find a map showing the location of the Pisgah District relative to the rest of North Carolina as well as an area map indicating where you'll find the start/finish for each route.

- The **Regional Information** section has several subsections that will give you information on places to stay in the area, where bike shops are located, and what kind of weather you can expect at different times of the year.

Mountain Bike Etiquette

The old phrase "use it or lose it" has never been more true than in the case of mountain biking on public and private lands. In this case it's more appropriate to say "use it *properly* or lose it." It takes only a few incidents of irresponsible or abusive trail riding to close a trail, a recreation area or an entire national forest to mountain bikers. For years now the **International Mountain Biking Association (I.M.B.A.)** has been promoting mountain bicycling opportunities through environmentally and socially responsible use of the land. Below are the I.M.B.A. rules of the trail:

- Ride on open trails only.

- Leave no trace.

- Control your bicycle.

- Always yield trail.

- Never spook animals.

- Plan ahead.

Joining I.M.B.A. is easy, inexpensive and highly recommended. Memberships are available for individuals, clubs and businesses. For more information contact:

International Mountain Biking Association
P.O. Box 7578
Boulder, CO 80306
303/545-9011

Riding in the Pisgah National Forest

Blaze Color

More Difficult

C
L
U
B

G
A
P

The national forests in North Carolina provide excellent opportunities for mountain bike use. This is especially the case in the Pisgah District of the Pisgah National Forest, where trails are well marked and specifically designated for all uses, including bikes. You'll quickly learn to look for the familiar trail or road markers at all trail heads and trail junctions.

Currently, the trails policy for North Carolina national forests is: "Driving, riding, possessing, parking or leaving any kind of transportation on a developed trail not designated, and so posted for that specific use" is prohibited. This means that mountain bikes are allowed only on trails posted for their use and any developed trail without such a sign should be considered closed to bikes. Bikes are allowed on gated and closed Forest Service roads, unless posted otherwise.

At the date of this publication, all the trails and roads listed here are open to bikes year round, with the exception of the seasonal trails. Seasonal trails are open to bikes from October 15 to April 15 only. In the event that excessive resource damage occurs on a specific trail or visitor safety considerations arise, it is possible that some trails will be closed. It is also possible that in the future more trails may be opened or that seasonal trails will be considered for year round use. Obviously, it is important that all mountain bikers stay only on open trails and use their best trail etiquette. In this way, the good image of bikers that exists in Pisgah will be maintained for years to come.

For up-to-date trail information, to volunteer a group for trail building or maintenance, to inquire about scouting new routes, or to make suggestions for future mountain biking opportunities, contact:

Pisgah District Ranger Office
1001 Pisgah Highway
Pisgah Forest, NC 28768
704/877-3265

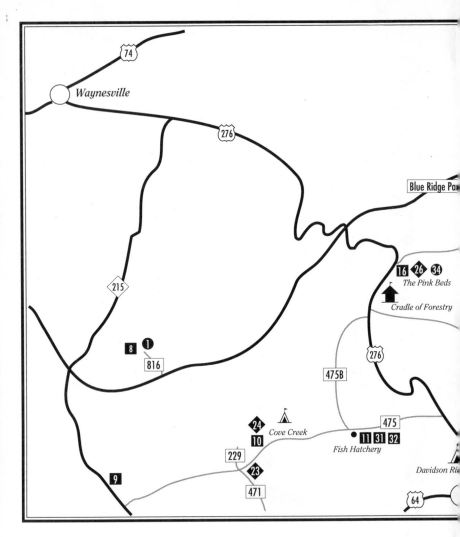

74

Waynesville

276

Blue Ridge Pa

215

16 26 34
The Pink Beds

Cradle of Forestry

8 1

276

816

475B

24
Cove Creek

475

10
229

11 31 32
Fish Hatchery

23

Davidson Ri

9

471

64

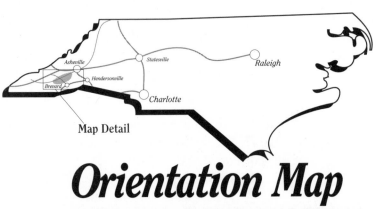

Asheville   Statesville   Raleigh

Hendersonville

Brevard

Charlotte

Map Detail

Orientation Map

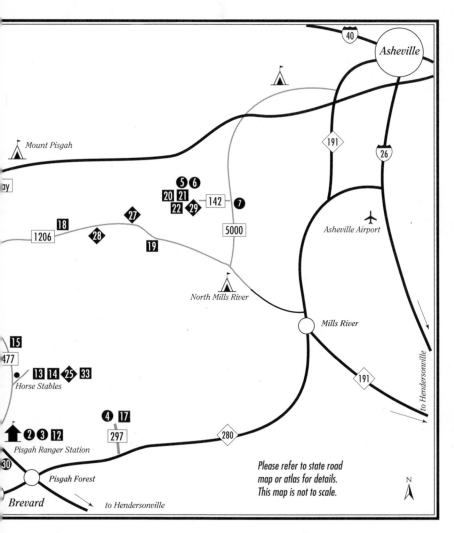

● Easiest Trails

1. *Ivestor Gap*
2. *Thrift Cove*
3. *Sycamore Cove*
4. *Old Cantrell Creek Lodge*
5. *Wash Creek*
6. *Fletcher Creek*
7. *Bear Branch*

■ More Difficult Trails

8. *Flat Laurel Creek*
9. *Summey Cove*
10. *Daniel Ridge*

11. *Gumstand Gap*
12. *Pressley Gap*
13. *Twin Falls*
14. *Buckhorn Gap*
15. *Buckwheat Knob*
16. *Club Gap*
17. *Riverside*
18. *Slate Rock Creek*
19. *Bradley Creek*
20. *Spencer Gap*
21. *Spencer Branch*
22. *Middle Fork*

◆ Most Difficult Trails

23. *Pilot Mountain*
24. *Farlow Gap*
25. *Clawhammer*
26. *Mountains To Mills River*
27. *Laurel Mountain*
28. *South Mills Tour*
29. *Trace Ridge*

Seasonal Trails

30. *North Slope*
31. *Butter Gap*
32. *Picklesimer Fields*
33. *Bennett Gap*
34. *The Pink Beds*

EASIEST TRAILS

❶ *Ivestor Gap*

Bordering the Shining Rock Wilderness, this rocky old road bed traverses the high ridges above Wash Hollow and Graveyard Fields. Blueberries abound in late August.

Start/Finish
Trailhead parking area for Black Balsam at end of FS 816 off Blue Ridge Parkway.

Highlights
No hills, very rocky, slow riding, high meadows, waterfall, berries in season, wet areas

Trail Configuration
Out-and-Back

Total Distance
8 miles

Surface
Double track • 8 miles

Time Allowance
Beginner • 3 hours
Intermediate • 2.5 hours
Advanced • 2 hours

Mileposts

- **From start**–ride through gate out Ivestor Gap Trail (the gate to this old road is open from mid-August through December for berry pickers and hunters).
- **Mile 1.6**– junction Art Loeb Trail. Stay left on old road.
- **Mile 2.0**– Ivestor Gap and Wilderness boundary **(no bikes are allowed in wilderness areas)**. Follow old road to right of Wilderness Area.
- **Mile 2.3**– take a sharp right turn onto Graveyard Ridge Trail.
- **Mile 2.9**– waterfall to left (if you don't see it, you can hear it).
- **Mile 4.0**– deep washout. Road bed turns into foot trail. Turn around; **bikes are not allowed on the trail from here to Graveyard Fields and the Blue Ridge Parkway**.
- **Mile 8.0**– finish.

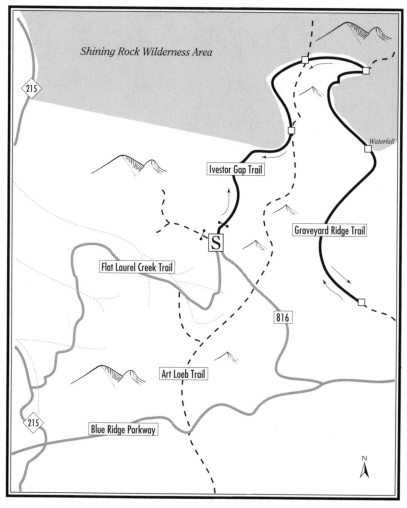

Shining Rock Wilderness Area

215

Ivestor Gap Trail

Waterfall

Graveyard Ridge Trail

S

Flat Laurel Creek Trail

816

Art Loeb Trail

215

Blue Ridge Parkway

N

MAP KEY

Bike Route......................... ∿

Other Trail or Road........... ∿

Direction of Travel............... →

Start/Finish..................... S

Milepost.......................... □

Public Land......................

Other Land......................

Recreation/Camping Area... ⛺

Major Mountain..................

River, Lake or Stream.....

Forest Service Rd. #................ 476

Road or Trail Name..... Black Mountain Trail

Foot Travel Only....... - - - - -

Timber Cut or Clearing.. ////////

5800'

5360'

Elevation Change

② Thrift Cove

Only minutes from the ranger station, this trail works its way slowly up the cove on a grassy logging road before returning by way of the Black Mountain Trail along Thrift Creek. You can double your distance by combining this with the Sycamore Cove Trail via Grass Road.

Start/Finish

Pisgah District Ranger Station on U.S. 276.

Trail Configuration

Loop

Surface

Single track • 4 miles
Pavement • 0.5 miles

Highlights

Grassy surface, fern glades, meadows, mud bogs, rhododendron tunnels, open woods

Total Distance

4.5 miles

Time Allowance

Beginner • 1.5 hours
Intermediate • 1 hour
Advanced • 30 minutes

Mileposts

- **From start**– ride south (left) on U.S. 276.
- **Mile 0.3**– turn left into parking area just past work center and continue onto Black Mountain Trail.
- **Mile 0.5**– Black Mountain Trail turns off to left. Turn right on Thrift Cove Trail **(red blaze)**.
- **Mile 0.6**– cross meadow. Mountains to Sea Trail crosses and then 100 yds. further the trail forks. The right fork is Grass Road. Take the left fork. This is Thrift Cove Trail.
- **Mile 2.8**– bear left on Black Mountain Trail **(white blaze)**.
- **Mile 4.1**– turn right on old road bed.
- **Mile 4.2**– Turn right on U.S. 276.
- **Mile 4.5**– finish.

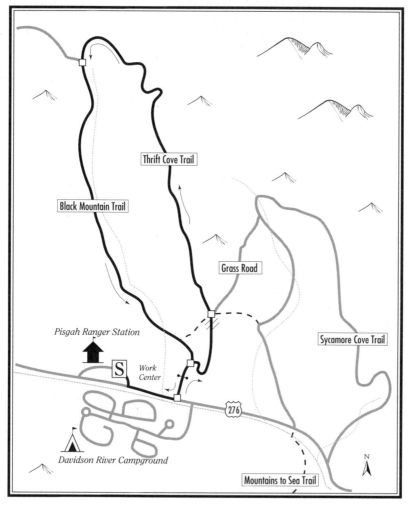

MAP KEY

Bike Route............................. ～

Other Trail or Road........... ～

Direction of Travel................ →

Start/Finish............................ ⑤

Milepost................................. ▫

Public Land......................

Other Land......................

Recreation/Camping Area... ⛺

Major Mountain..................

River, Lake or Stream.....

Forest Service Rd. #................. 476

Road or Trail Name..... Black Mountain Trail

Foot Travel Only....... ﹘ ﹘ ﹘

Timber Cut or Clearing.. //////

2920'

2160'

Elevation Change

Sycamore Cove

This is the first trail you come to as you enter the national forest from Brevard on U.S. 276. It climbs quickly up through a fern glade to the ridgeline and then rolls slowly downward along the ridge on an old road bed before dropping suddenly back to the highway.

Start/Finish
Pisgah District Ranger Station on U.S. 276.

Trail Configuration
Loop

Surface
Single track • 3.2 miles
Pavement • 1.5 miles

Highlights
Log bridges, ridge riding, rhododendron tunnels, log steps, steep downhill

Total Distance
4.7 miles

Time Allowance
Beginner • 1.5 hours
Intermediate • 1.25 hours
Advanced • 45 minutes

Mileposts

- **From start**– ride south (left) on U.S. 276.
- **Mile 0.6**– turn left onto Sycamore Cove Trail **(blue blaze)**. The Mountains to Sea Trail shares this trail for a ways, so you will also see a **round white blaze**.
- **Mile 1.2**– Mountains to Sea Trail exits to left. Stay on Sycamore Cove Trail.
- **Mile 1.9**– Grass Road enters from left. Stay on Sycamore Cove Trail.
- **Mile 3.8**– turn right on U.S. 276.
- **Mile 4.7**– finish.

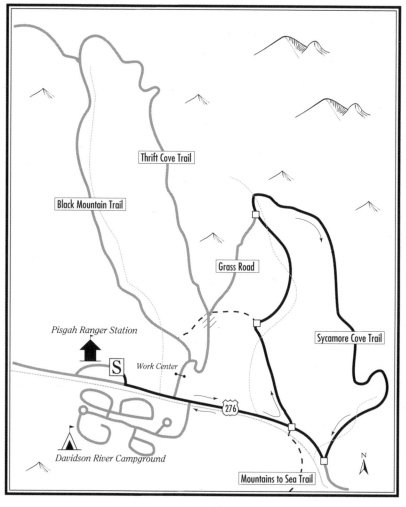

Thrift Cove Trail

Black Mountain Trail

Grass Road

Pisgah Ranger Station

Sycamore Cove Trail

Work Center

S

276

Davidson River Campground

N

Mountains to Sea Trail

MAP KEY

Bike Route..........................	～
Other Trail or Road...........	～
Direction of Travel...............	→
Start/Finish............................	S
Milepost..................................	□
Public Land......................	▭
Other Land........................	▬
Recreation/Camping Area...	⛺
Major Mountain..................	🏔
River, Lake or Stream.....	

Forest Service Rd. #.................	476
Road or Trail Name.....	Black Mountain Trail
Foot Travel Only........	- - -
Timber Cut or Clearing..	⁄⁄⁄⁄

2600'

2160'

Elevation Change

Old Cantrell Creek Lodge

Easy, with a few hills and several suspension bridge river crossings, this ride takes you up the South Mills River to an old lodge chimney. Built in 1890, the historic lodge itself was moved in 1970 to its present location at the Cradle of Forestry.

Start/Finish

Trailhead at northern end of FS 297. FS 297 is located off NC 280, 5 miles east of the NC 280/US 276 jct. in Pisgah Forest.

Trail Configuration

Out-and-Back

Surface

Single track • 7.2 miles

Highlights

Suspension bridges, historic site, heavy horse use, swimming holes, wide trail

Total Distance

7.2 miles

Time Allowance

Beginner • 2 hours
Intermediate • 1.5 hours
Advanced • 1 hour

Mileposts

- **From start**– ride through gate and down roadbed to right on South Mills River Trail.
- **Mile 0.8**– 4-way trails jct. Turn left and ride 0.1 mile upstream and cross river on swinging bridge.
- **Mile 1.0**– turn left up the hill on South Mills River Trail **(white blaze)**.
- **Mile 1.3**– Mullinax Trail enters on right.
- **Mile 1.6**– Pounding Mill Trail enters on right.
- **Mile 2.6**– cross river on swinging bridge.
- **Mile 2.8**– Wagon Road Gap Trail enters from left.
- **Mile 3.4**– cross river on swinging bridge.
- **Mile 3.6**– site of Cantrell Creek Lodge. There is a historical sign by the old chimney. Turn around here.
- **Mile 7.2**– finish.

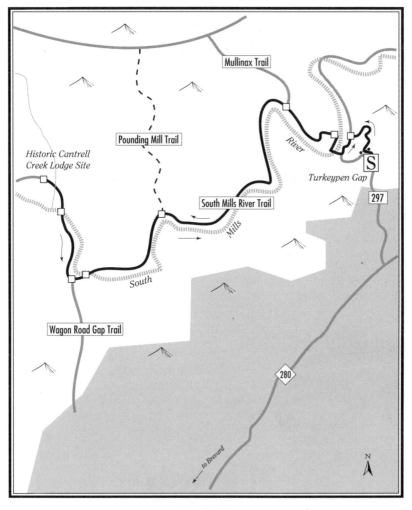

Mullinax Trail

Pounding Mill Trail

Historic Cantrell
Creek Lodge Site

Turkeypen Gap

River

South Mills River Trail

Mills

South

Wagon Road Gap Trail

297

280

to Brevard

N

MAP KEY

Bike Route...........................	～	Forest Service Rd. #.................	476
Other Trail or Road...........	～	Road or Trail Name.....	Black Mountain Trail
Direction of Travel...............	→	Foot Travel Only.......	- - - -
Start/Finish............................	S	Timber Cut or Clearing..	/////
Milepost..................................	□		
Public Land......................			
Other Land......................			
Recreation/Camping Area...	▲		
Major Mountain..................			
River, Lake or Stream.....			

2640'

2400'

Elevation Change

⑤

Wash Creek

A great ride for the beginner who wants a try at single track riding. It's short and all the single track is downhill. This is also a nice addition to any of the other rides in the Fletcher Creek area.

Start/Finish

To get to the trailhead, drive north for 2 miles on FS 5000 from North Mills River Campground and then turn left on FS 142 for 0.5 miles.

Trail Configuration

Loop

Surface

Single track • 1.3 miles
Forest road • 0.5 miles

Highlights

Short, the single track is all downhill, horse use

Total Distance

1.8 miles

Time Allowance

Beginner • 30 minutes
Intermediate • 20 minutes
Advanced • 15 minutes

Mileposts

- **From start–** ride downhill on Trace Ridge Trail **(orange blazes)**.
- **Mile 0.4–** turn sharply back to left on Wash Creek Trail **(yellow blazes)**. It's easy to miss this turn, so be on the lookout.
- **Mile 1.3–** turn left on FS 142.
- **Mile 1.8–** finish.

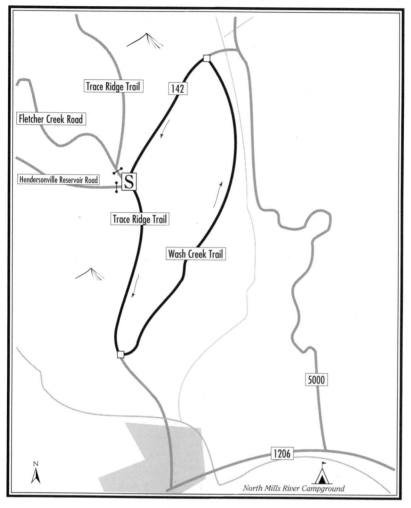

Trace Ridge Trail

Fletcher Creek Road

142

Hendersonville Reservoir Road

S

Trace Ridge Trail

Wash Creek Trail

5000

1206

N

North Mills River Campground

MAP KEY

Bike Route........................... ∿	Forest Service Rd. #................. 476
Other Trail or Road........... ∿	Road or Trail Name..... Black Mountain Trail
Direction of Travel................ →	Foot Travel Only........ - - - - -
Start/Finish............................ S	Timber Cut or Clearing.. /////
Milepost.................................. □	
Public Land...................... ▭	
Other Land...................... ▭	
Recreation/Camping Area... ⛺	2560'
Major Mountain.................. ⛰	2400'
River, Lake or Stream.....	**Elevation Change**

Fletcher Creek

This is a great ride for all ability levels. Starting on what is known by the locals as the "Never Ending Road," you'll ride out to the headwaters of Fletcher Creek and then you and the stream will build up steam together as you return on a beautiful trail.

Start/Finish

To get to the trailhead, drive north for 2 miles on FS 5000 from North Mills River Campground and then turn left on FS 142 for 0.5 miles.

Trail Configuration

Loop

Surface

Single track • 2.3 miles
Forest road • 6.8 miles

Highlights

Gravel road cruising, few small hills, creek crossing, open woods, meadows, horse use

Total Distance

9.1 miles

Time Allowance

Beginner • 2 hours
Intermediate • 1.5 hours
Advanced • 1 hour

Mileposts

- **From start**– ride through gate and out Fletcher Creek Road.
- **Mile 4.6**– Spencer Branch Trail crosses road.
- **Mile 5.6**– turn left onto Fletcher Creek Trail **(blue blaze)**.
- **Mile 6.4**– trail crosses big meadow.
- **Mile 6.8**– Middle Fork Trail enters from right. Cross Fletcher Creek and intersect Spencer Branch Trail. Continue straight on Fletcher Creek Trail.
- **Mile 7.9**– turn left on Hendersonville Reservoir Road.
- **Mile 9.1**– finish.

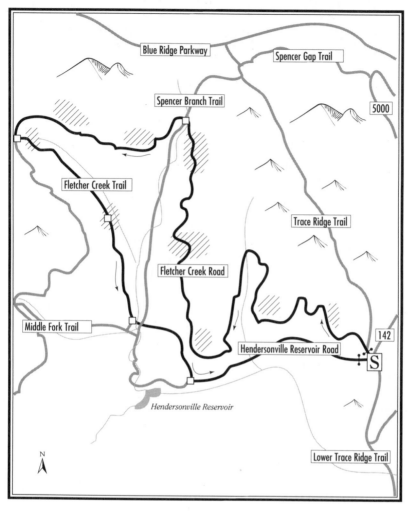

MAP KEY

Bike Route........................	~	Forest Service Rd. #.................	476
Other Trail or Road...........	~	Road or Trail Name.....	Black Mountain Trail
Direction of Travel................	→	Foot Travel Only........	- - -
Start/Finish...........................	S	Timber Cut or Clearing..	/////
Milepost................................	□		
Public Land......................			
Other Land......................			
Recreation/Camping Area...	⛺		
Major Mountain..................	⛰		
River, Lake or Stream.....			

Elevation Change

2560'

2480'

22

Bear Branch

As you meander through a somewhat confusing network of trails, you'll notice that blue-blazed trails seem to head off in all directions. This is the best and easiest route through the maze. Pay close attention to the mileposts!

Start/Finish

2 miles north on FS 5000 from North Mills River Campground, just across from FS 142.

Trail Configuration

Loop with extension

Surface

Single track • 2.1 miles
Forest road • 0.8 miles

Highlights

Horse use, hidden turns, blazed and unblazed trail network, small streams, rocky in places

Total Distance

2.9 miles

Time Allowance

Beginner • 1 hour
Intermediate • 45 minutes
Advanced • 20 minutes

Mileposts

- **From start**– ride over whoop-te-doos just to left of gate onto Bear Branch Loop Trail **(blue blaze)**. The steep, seldom used Bear Branch Trail exits immediately to the left.
- **Mile 0.5**– bear left at fork to begin the loop.
- **Mile 0.6**– turn left onto woods road.
- **Mile 0.8**– turn right onto Seniard Mountain Road.
- **Mile 1.6**– turn right onto Bear Branch Loop Trail.
- **Mile 1.8**– trail forks. Bear right down the hill.
- **Mile 2.0**– turn right on **blue-blazed** woods road and then immediately left on trail after crossing bridge.
- **Mile 2.2**– bear left as you close the loop.
- **Mile 2.9**– finish.

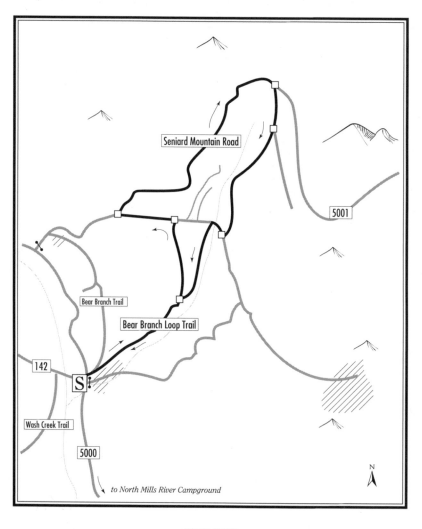

Seniard Mountain Road

5001

Bear Branch Trail

Bear Branch Loop Trail

142

S

Wash Creek Trail

5000

to North Mills River Campground

N

MAP KEY

Bike Route.......................... ～	Forest Service Rd. #................. 476
Other Trail or Road........... ～	Road or Trail Name..... Black Mountain Trail
Direction of Travel............... →	Foot Travel Only....... - - - -
Start/Finish............................ S	Timber Cut or Clearing.. ////
Milepost................................. □	
Public Land...................... ▭	
Other Land...................... ▭	
Recreation/Camping Area... ⛺	
Major Mountain..................	
River, Lake or Stream.....	

2800'

2428'

Elevation Change

MORE DIFFICULT TRAILS

Flat Laurel Creek

Starting in the high meadows between Shining Rock and the Middle Prong Wilderness, this ride connects with the Blue Ridge Parkway. The entire ride is above 5000 feet.

Start/Finish

Trailhead parking area for Black Balsam at end of FS 816 off the Blue Ridge Parkway.

Trail Configuration

Loop

Surface

Single track • 2.6 miles
Pavement • 4.6 miles

Highlights

Waterfalls, creek crossings, cliff views, high meadows, rocky trail, Blue Ridge Parkway, Devil's Courthouse tunnel

Total Distance

7.2 miles

Time Allowance

Beginner • 3 hours
Intermediate • 2.25 hours
Advanced • 1.5 hours

Special Note: *Front lights and rear reflectors are required for riding bicycles through tunnels on the Blue Ridge Parkway.*

Mileposts

- **From start**– ride out back of parking lot onto Flat Laurel Creek Trail. The first mile is very rocky.
- **Mile 0.9**– cross creek and turn right.
- **Mile 1.1**– look for the waterfall on your right just after passing a flat camping spot.
- **Mile 2.3**– cross old concrete bridge. You'll see a waterfall on the left, just above the bridge.
- **Mile 2.6**– cross creek and turn left onto NC 215.
- **Mile 3.0**– turn left onto Blue Ridge Parkway.
- **Mile 4.0**– Devil's Courthouse and tunnel.
- **Mile 6.0**– turn left onto FS 816 to Black Balsam.
- **Mile 7.2**– finish.

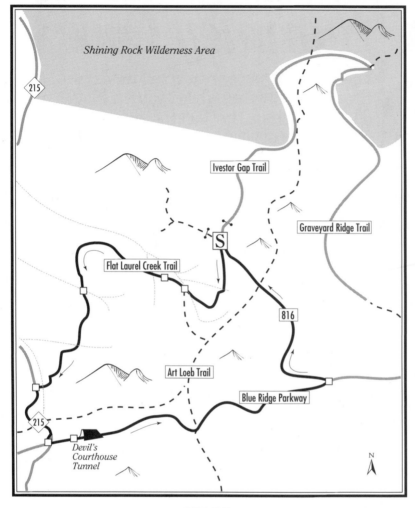

Shining Rock Wilderness Area

215

Ivestor Gap Trail

Graveyard Ridge Trail

S

Flat Laurel Creek Trail

816

Art Loeb Trail

Blue Ridge Parkway

215

Devil's
Courthouse
Tunnel

N

MAP KEY

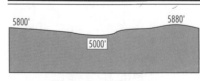

Bike Route...................... 〜	Forest Service Rd. #................. 476
Other Trail or Road........... 〜	Road or Trail Name..... Black Mountain Trail
Direction of Travel............... →	Foot Travel Only....... - - - -
Start/Finish............................ S	Timber Cut or Clearing.. /////
Milepost.................................... □	
Public Land...................... ▢	
Other Land...................... ▢	
Recreation/Camping Area... ▲	
Major Mountain.................. 〜	
River, Lake or Stream..... 〜	

5800'   5880'

5000'

Elevation Change

Summey Cove

Following the upper reaches of the French Broad River, this route takes you to a hidden 60-foot waterfall. Don't let the distance fool you; there is one very steep hill climb.

Start/Finish

Jct. of NC 215 and FS 140. This is 6.6 miles south of the Blue Ridge Parkway and one mile north of Balsam Grove on NC 215.

Trail Configuration

Loop

Surface

Single track • 1.6 miles
Forest road • 3 miles
Pavement • 1.4 miles

Highlights

Cascades, Courthouse Falls, very steep uphill and downhill, great views

Total Distance

6 miles

Time Allowance

Beginner • 3.5 hours
Intermediate • 2.5 hours
Advanced • 1.5 hours

Mileposts

- **From start**– ride north up FS 140.
- **Mile 0.8**– FS 140A enters from right, stay left beside river.
- **Mile 2.6**– Kiesee Creek Road enters from right. Bear left, downhill.
- **Mile 3.0**– bottom of hill. Cross bridge and turn left onto Summey Cove Trail **(white blazes)**.
- **Mile 3.3**– Courthouse Falls Trail turns off to left. (it's a short hike to base of the falls—**foot travel only**).
- **Mile 4.1**– cross creek and start steep hill climb.
- **Mile 4.2**– cross logging road.
- **Mile 4.6**– jct. NC 215, turn left.
- **Mile 6**– finish.

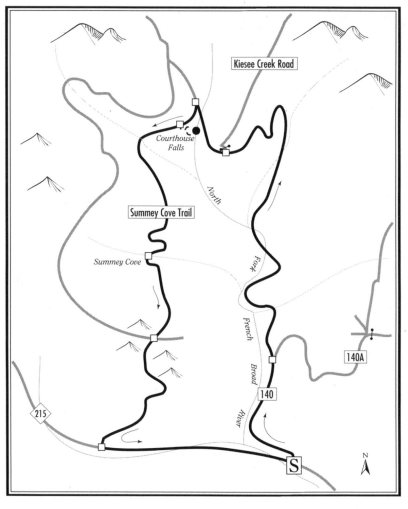

Kiesee Creek Road

Courthouse Falls

North

Summey Cove Trail

Summey Cove

Fork

French

Broad

140A

140

River

215

S

N

MAP KEY

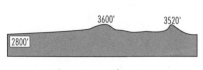

Bike Route........................ ∼	Forest Service Rd. #................. 476
Other Trail or Road........... ∼	Road or Trail Name..... Black Mountain Trail
Direction of Travel................ →	Foot Travel Only........ - - -
Start/Finish........................... S	Timber Cut or Clearing.. /////
Milepost.................................. □	

Public Land.....................

Other Land.......................

Recreation/Camping Area... ⛺

Major Mountain.................

River, Lake or Stream.....

3600'   3520'

2800'

Elevation Change

Daniel Ridge

It's a bit of a push to the ridge, but once you're there the extra effort is long forgotten. The grassy woods, open meadows and cliff-top views heighten your senses, while some technical riding sharpens your skills.

Start/Finish

Parking area 0.8 miles west of entrance to Cove Creek Group Camp on FS 475.

Trail Configuration

Loop

Surface

Single track • 3.5 miles
Forest road • 0.6 miles

Highlights

Roots, log bridges, waterfall, steep hills, mud bogs, short push, grassy woods, meadows

Total Distance

4.1 miles

Time Allowance

Beginner • 2 hours
Intermediate • 1.25 hours
Advanced • 45 minutes

Mileposts

- **From start**– ride through gate on unmarked FS 137.
- **Mile 0.1**– cross bridge, go 25 yds. and turn left onto Daniel Ridge Trail **(red blazes)**.
- **Mile 0.6**– trail forks. Take the right fork.
- **Mile 1.3**– trail forks just before old log bridge. Take right fork up hill **(red blazes)**. The next 0.3 miles is pretty steep.
- **Mile 1.6**– turn right at jct. of Farlow Gap Trail. You are still on the Daniel Ridge Trail **(red blazes)**.
- **Mile 2.5**– cross logging road.
- **Mile 3.2**– look and listen for waterfall to left of trail.
- **Mile 3.6**– turn right onto FS 5046.
- **Mile 4.1**– finish.

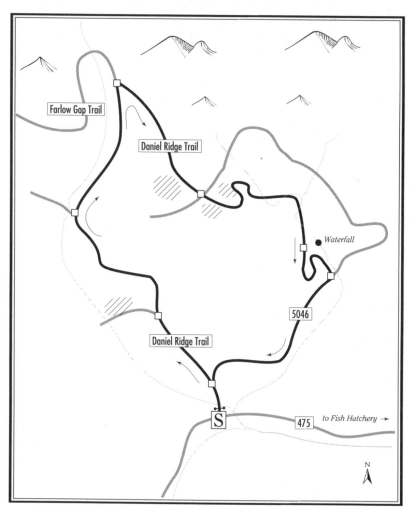

Farlow Gap Trail

Daniel Ridge Trail

Waterfall

5046

Daniel Ridge Trail

S

475 to Fish Hatchery →

N

MAP KEY

Bike Route..........................	~	
Other Trail or Road...........	~	
Direction of Travel...............	→	
Start/Finish.............................	S	
Milepost...................................	□	
Public Land......................	▭	
Other Land......................	▬	
Recreation/Camping Area...	⛺	
Major Mountain....................		
River, Lake or Stream.....		

Forest Service Rd. #.................	476
Road or Trail Name.....	Black Mountain Trail
Foot Travel Only........	- - - -
Timber Cut or Clearing..	/////

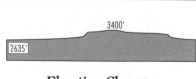

3400'

2635'

Elevation Change

11

Gumstand Gap

With views of Looking Glass Rock, John Rock and several high waterfalls, this is an appealing scenic ride. Throw in three miles of great single track and you've got something special.

Start/Finish
State Fish Hatchery on FS 475.

Trail Configuration
Loop

Surface
Single track • 2.7 miles
Forest road • 7.1 miles

Highlights
Rhododendron tunnels, waterfalls, cliff views, creek crossings

Total Distance
9.8 miles

Time Allowance
Beginner • 2.5 hours
Intermediate • 1.75 hours
Advanced • 1.25 hours

Mileposts

- **From start**– cross bridge and turn left out of fish hatchery parking lot onto FS 475.
- **Mile 0.2**– turn right onto FS 475B.
- **Mile 3.7**– Gumstand Gap. Turn left onto FS 225. In the next mile, numerous unmarked roads and trails will enter on either side. Stay on FS 225.
- **Mile 4.6**– turn left onto gated road. This is the Caney Bottom Extension Trail (marked by a sign). Go 50 yards and the trail forks off to the right **(yellow blazes)**. Turn right onto the trail.
- **Mile 5.1**– Caney Bottom Trail. Turn right **(blue blazes)**.
- **Mile 5.7**– yellow blazed trail enters from right.
- **Mile 7.3**– bypass Cove Creek Group Camp. Turn right onto road.
- **Mile 7.8**– turn left onto FS 475.
- **Mile 9.8**– finish.

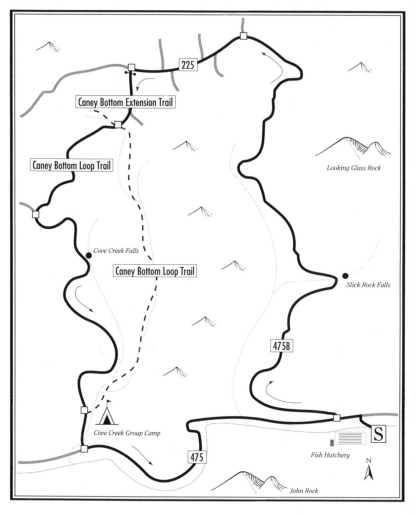

Caney Bottom Extension Trail

Caney Bottom Loop Trail

Caney Bottom Loop Trail

Cove Creek Falls

Cove Creek Group Camp

225

475B

475

Looking Glass Rock

Slick Rock Falls

Fish Hatchery

S

John Rock

N

MAP KEY

Bike Route.......................... ∿

Other Trail or Road........... ∿

Direction of Travel................ ⟶

Start/Finish............................ [S]

Milepost.................................. ▫

Public Land.......................

Other Land.......................

Recreation/Camping Area... ⛺

Major Mountain...................

River, Lake or Stream.....

Forest Service Rd. #.................. 476

Road or Trail Name..... Black Mountain Trail

Foot Travel Only........ ⌐ ⌐ ⌐ ⌐

Timber Cut or Clearing.. ⫽⫽⫽

3280'

2370'

Elevation Change

12

Pressley Gap

Starting and finishing at the ranger station, this ride combines easy streamside riding with a 4-mile climb and good technical downhill single track.

Start/Finish

Pisgah District Ranger Station on U.S . 276.

Trail Configuration

Loop

Surface

Single track • 2.9 miles
Double track • 1.4 miles
Forest road • 4 miles
Pavement • 1 mile

Highlights

Views, timber cuts, some horse use, grassy road, diagonal log water breaks, short pushes

Total Distance

9.3 miles

Time Allowance

Beginner • 5 hours
Intermediate • 3.5 hours
Advanced • 2.5 hours

Mileposts

- **From start**– ride west on FS 276.
- **Mile 0.7**– turn right onto FS 477. You should see a sign pointing to the horseback riding area.
- **Mile 2.4**– Horse stables. Turn right on gated Clawhammer Road.
- **Mile 3.5**– turn right onto gated Maxwell Cove Road.
- **Mile 4.7**– unmarked road to left. Continue right up Maxwell Cove Road (it becomes grassy).
- **Mile 6.1**– Pressley Gap. 5-way junction. Take a sharp right onto Black Mountain/Mountains to Sea Trail **(white blaze w/ white dot)**.
- **Mile 7.5**– Thrift Cove Trail enters from left.
- **Mile 8.6**– Mountains to Sea Trail exits to left.
- **Mile 8.7**– Thrift Cove Trail enters from left.
- **Mile 9.0**– turn right and pass work station on US 276.
- **Mile 9.3**– finish.

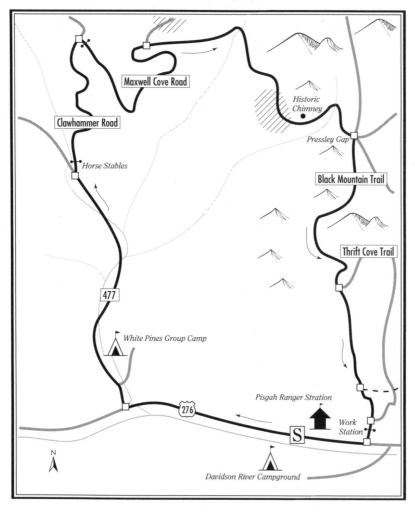

Maxwell Cove Road

Clawhammer Road

Historic Chimney

Pressley Gap

Black Mountain Trail

Horse Stables

Thrift Cove Trail

477

White Pines Group Camp

Pisgah Ranger Stration

Work Station

S

N

Davidson River Campground

276

MAP KEY

Bike Route.......................... 〜

Other Trail or Road........... 〜

Direction of Travel............... ⟶

Start/Finish............................. Ⓢ

Milepost.................................. □

Public Land......................

Other Land.......................

Recreation/Camping Area... ⛺

Major Mountain....................

River, Lake or Stream.....

Forest Service Rd. #................. 476

Road or Trail Name..... Black Mountain Trail

Foot Travel Only........ - - - - -

Timber Cut or Clearing.. //////

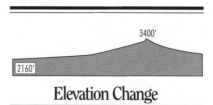

3400'

2160'

Elevation Change

13

Twin Falls

A gem in the Avery Creek system. You'll double your visual pleasure as this ride takes you within a short hike of a double waterfall. Two creeks tumble over a cliff side by side.

Start/Finish

Horseback riding area on FS 477 1.5 miles north of White Pines Group Camp.

Trail Configuration

Loop

Surface

Single track • 2.7 miles
Forest road • 3.4 miles

Highlights

Views, twin waterfalls, log bridges, few short carries, horse fords, long uphill on gravel road, horse use

Total Distance

6.1 miles

Time Allowance

Beginner • 3 hours
Intermediate • 2 hours
Advanced • 1.5 hours

Mileposts

- **From start**– ride through gate up Clawhammer Road.
- **Mile 1.0**– Maxwell Cove Road enters from right. Stay left on Clawhammer Road.
- **Mile 2.6**– a grassy meadow (old cemetery) on the left marks the entrance onto Buckhorn Gap Trail. Turn left down grassy road bed **(orange blazes)**.
- **Mile 3.5**– Buckhorn Gap Trail goes in two directions off of road bed. Turn left down the creek following **orange blazes**.
- **Mile 3.7**– **hiker-only** trail to Twin Falls turns off to right. Leave your bike here to make the short hike to the falls.
- **Mile 4.9**– ford creek and jct. Avery Creek Trail. Take Upper Avery Creek Trail to the right **(yellow blaze)**.
- **Mile 5.3**– turn left onto FS 477 (downhill).
- **Mile 6.1**– finish.

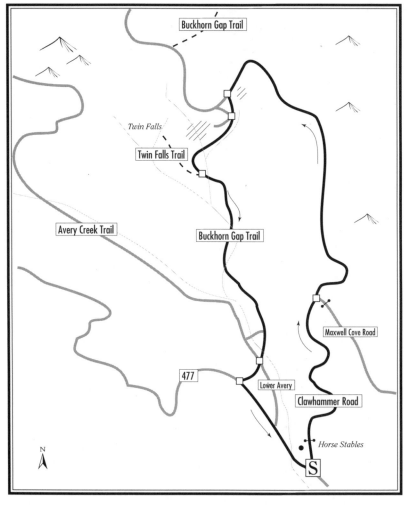

MAP KEY

Bike Route..........................	Forest Service Rd. #................. 476
Other Trail or Road...........	Road or Trail Name..... Black Mountain Trail
Direction of Travel............... →	Foot Travel Only....... - - - - -
Start/Finish............................ S	Timber Cut or Clearing.. /////////
Milepost.................................. □	
Public Land......................	
Other Land......................	
Recreation/Camping Area... ⚑	
Major Mountain...................	
River, Lake or Stream.....	

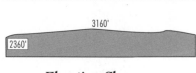

Elevation Change

3160'

2360'

14

Buckhorn Gap

If you can take the four-mile climb at the beginning in stride, you'll love the ridge ride that follows. In places the mountain falls off on both sides only a few feet from the trail.

Start/Finish

Horseback riding area on FS 477 north of White Pines Group Camp.

Highlights

Great views, horse use, log bridges, ridge riding, Buckhorn Gap Shelter, waterfalls, mud bogs

Trail Configuration

Loop

Total Distance

10.1 miles

Surface

Single track • 4.9 miles
Forest road • 5.2 miles

Time Allowance

Beginner • 4 hours
Intermediate • 3 hours
Advanced • 2 hours

Mileposts

- **From start**– ride through gate up Clawhammer Road.
- **Mile 1.0**– Maxwell Cove Road enters from right.
- **Mile 2.6**– Buckhorn Gap Trail enters from left.
- **Mile 3.6**– Buckhorn Gap Trail exits to right.
- **Mile 3.8**– unmarked road enters left. Bear right.
- **Mile 4.4**– Buckhorn Gap. Jct. Black Mountain/Mountains to Sea Trail and Buckhorn Gap Trail. Turn left up steps onto Black Mountain/Mountains to Sea Trail **(white blazes)**.
- **Mile 4.5**– Buckhorn Gap Shelter.
- **Mile 5.3**– Mountains to Sea Trail exits to right.
- **Mile 6.1**– Club Gap. Turn left onto Avery Creek Trail **(blue blazes)**.
- **Mile 8.2**– Buckhorn Gap Trail enters from left.
- **Mile 8.3**– horse ford. Turn right onto Upper Avery Creek Trail **(yellow blazes)**.
- **Mile 9.3**– turn left onto FS 477.
- **Mile 10.1**– finish.

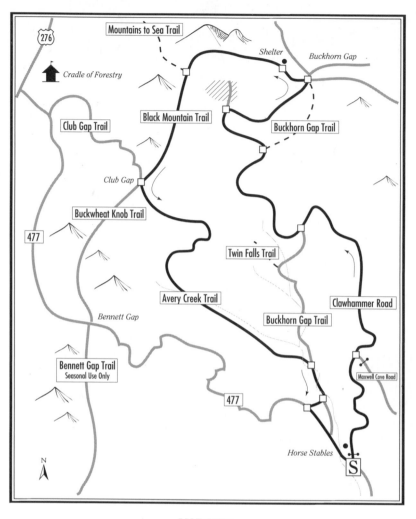

276

Cradle of Forestry

Mountains to Sea Trail

Shelter

Buckhorn Gap

Black Mountain Trail

Club Gap Trail

Buckhorn Gap Trail

Club Gap

477

Buckwheat Knob Trail

Twin Falls Trail

Avery Creek Trail

Clawhammer Road

Buckhorn Gap Trail

Bennett Gap

Bennett Gap Trail
Seasonal Use Only

Maxwell Cove Road

477

Horse Stables

S

N

MAP KEY

Bike Route.......................... ∿

Other Trail or Road........... ∿

Direction of Travel.............. ⟶

Start/Finish............................ ⑤

Milepost.................................. ▫

Public Land.......................

Other Land........................

Recreation/Camping Area... ⛺

Major Mountain.....................

River, Lake or Stream.....

Forest Service Rd. #................. 476

Road or Trail Name..... Black Mountain Trail

Foot Travel Only....... ⌐ ⌐ ⌐ ⌐

Timber Cut or Clearing.. ⫽⫽⫽

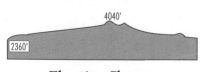

4040'

2360'

Elevation Change

15

Buckwheat Knob

The first three miles is mostly uphill and it takes some pushing to get over Buckwheat Knob, but the descent to the creek is a real treat. You'll enjoy the views from the gravel road.

Start/Finish

Trailhead at southern end of Upper Avery Creek Trail on FS 477, 0.8 miles from the horseback riding area.

Trail Configuration

Loop

Surface

Single track • 4.9 miles
Forest road • 2.3 miles

Highlights

Nice views, some pushing required, ruts, log bridges, mud bogs, waterfalls, horse use

Total Distance

7.2 miles

Time Allowance

Beginner • 3 hours
Intermediate • 2.25 hours
Advanced • 1.75 hours

Mileposts

- **From start**– ride northwest on FS 477 (uphill).
- **Mile 2.3**– Bennett Gap. Turn right onto Buckwheat Knob Trail **(yellow blaze)**.
- **Mile 3.8**– After climbing over two very steep knobs, you'll reach Club Gap. Turn right onto Avery Creek Trail **(blue blazes)**.
- **Mile 5.4**– listen for waterfall off left side of trail.
- **Mile 6.1**– Buckhorn Gap Trail enters from left.
- **Mile 6.2**– horse ford and trail splits. Bear right on Upper Avery Creek Trail **(yellow blaze)**.
- **Mile 7.2**– finish.

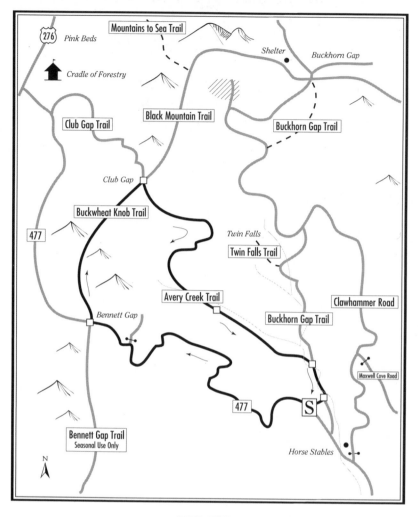

276 *Pink Beds*

Mountains to Sea Trail

Shelter

Buckhorn Gap

Cradle of Forestry

Club Gap Trail

Black Mountain Trail

Buckhorn Gap Trail

Club Gap

477

Buckwheat Knob Trail

Twin Falls

Twin Falls Trail

Avery Creek Trail

Clawhammer Road

Bennett Gap

Buckhorn Gap Trail

Maxwell Cove Road

477

S

Bennett Gap Trail
Seasonal Use Only

Horse Stables

N

MAP KEY

Bike Route........................... ∿	Forest Service Rd. #................. 476
Other Trail or Road........... ∿	Road or Trail Name..... Black Mountain Trail
Direction of Travel................ →	Foot Travel Only....... - - - - -
Start/Finish........................... S	Timber Cut or Clearing.. //////
Milepost.................................. □	
Public Land......................	
Other Land......................	
Recreation/Camping Area... ▲	
Major Mountain..................	
River, Lake or Stream.....	

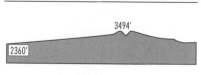

3494'

2360'

Elevation Change

16

Club Gap

Climbing steeply on single track from the historic Cradle of Forestry, this trail works its way up and over into the popular Avery Creek drainage area. A forest road with a fantastic view of Looking Glass Rock brings you back to the start.

Start/Finish

The Pink Beds parking area on U.S. 276.

Trail Configuration

Loop

Surface

Single track • 4.6 miles
Forest road • 5.1 miles
Pavement • 1 mile

Highlights

Some pushing, waterfall, views, log water breaks, the Pink Beds, Cradle of Forestry

Total Distance

10.7 miles

Time Allowance

Beginner • 3 hours
Intermediate • 2 hours
Advanced • 1.5 hours

Mileposts

- **From start**– ride south on U.S. 276 (left, downhill).
- **Mile 0.5**– turn left onto FS 477.
- **Mile 0.8**– take a sharp left on Club Gap Trail **(yellow blaze)**.
- **Mile 1.1**– turn right off the road bed up Club Gap Trail.
- **Mile 2.1**– Club Gap. Trails converge here. Continue straight (downhill) on Avery Creek Trail **(blue blaze)**.
- **Mile 4.4**– Buckhorn Gap Trail enters from left.
- **Mile 4.5**– horse ford. Turn right onto Upper Avery Trail **(yellow blaze)**.
- **Mile 5.4**– turn right onto FS 477.
- **Mile 8.2**– dramatic view of Looking Glass Rock to left.
- **Mile 9.9**– pass turn onto Club Gap Trail.
- **Mile 10.2**– turn right onto U.S. 276.
- **Mile 10.7**– finish.

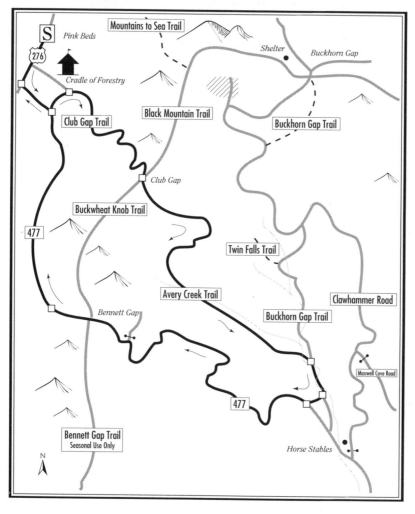

- S — Pink Beds
- 276
- Mountains to Sea Trail
- Shelter
- Buckhorn Gap
- Cradle of Forestry
- Black Mountain Trail
- Club Gap Trail
- Buckhorn Gap Trail
- Club Gap
- Buckwheat Knob Trail
- 477
- Twin Falls Trail
- Avery Creek Trail
- Clawhammer Road
- Bennett Gap
- Buckhorn Gap Trail
- Maxwell Cove Road
- 477
- Bennett Gap Trail
  Seasonal Use Only
- Horse Stables
- N

MAP KEY

Bike Route............................ 〜

Other Trail or Road........... 〜

Direction of Travel................ →

Start/Finish............................ S

Milepost................................. □

Public Land......................

Other Land......................

Recreation/Camping Area... ▲

Major Mountain.................

River, Lake or Stream.....

Forest Service Rd. #................. 476

Road or Trail Name..... Black Mountain Trail

Foot Travel Only....... ⌐ − ⌐ − ⌐

Timber Cut or Clearing.. ///////

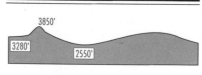

3850'

3280'

2550'

Elevation Change

44

17

Riverside

With 10 stream and river crossings, you're certain not to get overheated, and except for the short climb over Pea Gap, you never leave the water's edge. Take caution over the rooty and sandy sections.

Start/Finish

Trailhead at northern end of FS 297. FS 297 is located off NC 280, 5 miles east of the NC 280/US 276 jct. in Pisgah Forest.

Trail Configuration

Loop w/ extension

Surface

Single track • 7.8 miles

Highlights

River crossings, heavy horse use, sand and mud bogs, exposed roots

Total Distance

7.8 miles

Time Allowance

Beginner • 2.5 hours
Intermediate • 1.75 hours
Advanced • 1.25 hours

Mileposts

- **From start**– ride down the gated road located to the right of the South Mills River Trail.
- **Mile 0.8**– at river, turn sharply to the right onto the Bradley Creek Trail **(orange blaze)**.
- **Mile 1.6**– Riverside Trail enters from the right. Bear left (uphill) on Bradley Creek Trail **(orange blaze)**.
- **Mile 2.2**– Squirrel Gap Trail enters from the left.
- **Mile 2.8**– trail forks 100 feet after crossing a small stream. Take the right fork across Bradley Creek onto Vineyard Gap Trail **(yellow blaze)**.
- **Mile 3.8**– turn right onto Riverside Trail **(blue blaze)**, cross Bradley Creek and ride beside South Mills River.
- **Mile 5.9**– bear left onto Bradley Creek Trail **(orange blaze)** and finish the ride by returning the way you came.
- **Mile 7.8**– finish.

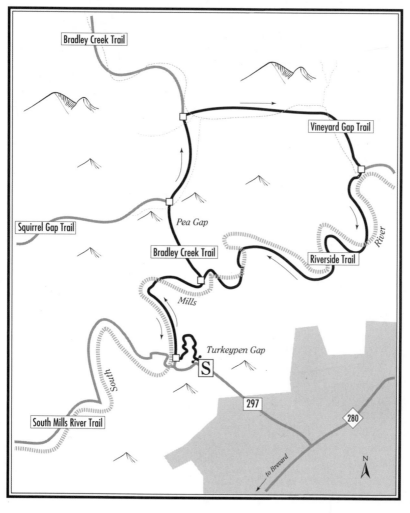

Bradley Creek Trail

Vineyard Gap Trail

Squirrel Gap Trail

Pea Gap

Bradley Creek Trail

Riverside Trail

River

Mills

Turkeypen Gap

S

South

297

280

South Mills River Trail

to Brevard

N

MAP KEY

Bike Route........................	∿	Forest Service Rd. #................	476
Other Trail or Road..........	∿	Road or Trail Name.....	Black Mountain Trail
Direction of Travel...............	→	Foot Travel Only.......	- - - -
Start/Finish....................	S	Timber Cut or Clearing..	/////
Milepost....................	□		
Public Land....................	▭		
Other Land....................	▬		
Recreation/Camping Area...	⛺		
Major Mountain.................	⛰		
River, Lake or Stream.....			

2640'

2300'

Elevation Change

18

Slate Rock Creek

This ride takes you up and over, through Pilot Cove to Slate Rock Creek. Along the way you'll pass several waterfalls and travel through lush and open fern-filled woods. You'll need to push some towards the top of Pilot Cove, but it's well worth the extra effort.

Start/Finish

There are two trailheads for the Pilot Cove/Slate Rock Creek Trail. Start at the one furthest west on FS 1206, 6.8 miles from North Mills River Campground.

Trail Configuration

Loop

Surface

Single track • 4.3 miles
Forest road • 1.7 miles

Highlights

Log bridges, fern glens, steep push, waterfalls, mud bogs, spotty views, short carries

Total Distance

6 miles

Time Allowance

Beginner • 3 hours
Intermediate • 2.25 hours
Advanced • 1.25 hours

Mileposts

- **From start**– ride up the Pilot Cove/Slate Rock Creek Trail **(blue blaze)**.
- **Mile 1.3**– top of Slate Rock Ridge.
- **Mile 2.0**– cross top of small waterfall.
- **Mile 3.4**– look for waterfall off right side of trail.
- **Mile 4.3**– turn right onto FS 1206.
- **Mile 6.0**– finish.

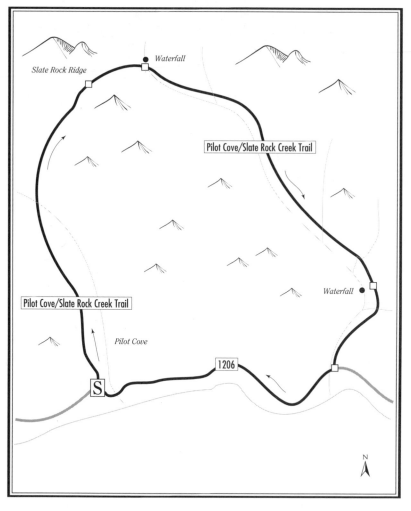

Slate Rock Ridge

Waterfall

Pilot Cove/Slate Rock Creek Trail

Pilot Cove/Slate Rock Creek Trail

Waterfall

Pilot Cove

1206

N

MAP KEY

Bike Route...........................	Forest Service Rd. #................. 476
Other Trail or Road...........	Road or Trail Name..... Black Mountain Trail
Direction of Travel..............	Foot Travel Only.......
Start/Finish............................ S	Timber Cut or Clearing..
Milepost.................................. □	
Public Land.....................	
Other Land......................	
Recreation/Camping Area...	
Major Mountain..................	
River, Lake or Stream.....	

3800'

3115'

2800'

Elevation Change

19

Bradley Creek

If you don't mind getting your feet wet, you'll love this ride. There are no fewer than twelve stream crossings. Don't worry—the ride on the gravel road back to the start will give your shoes plenty of time to dry out.

Start/Finish

Gate to FS 5015, 3.3 miles west of North Mills River Campground on FS 1206.

Highlights

Numerous stream crossings, mud bogs, timber cuts, views, cascades, bluff

Trail Configuration

Loop

Total Distance

7.0 miles

Surface

Single track • 1.6 miles
Forest road • 5.4 miles

Time Allowance

Beginner • 2.5 hours
Intermediate • 1.75 hours
Advanced • 1.25 hours

Mileposts

- **From start**– ride west on FS 1206 to the bottom of the hill.
- **Mile 1.5**– turn left onto Bradley Creek Trail **(orange blaze)**. This trail starts at the first pull-out on the left at the bottom of the hill. You immediately cross the creek and turn left downstream.
- **Mile 3.0**– bluff beside dam and small reservoir.
- **Mile 3.1**– enter timber cut and turn left (uphill) onto unmarked FS 5015. You'll ride through lots of timber cuts as you gradually climb the ridge back to the start.
- **Mile 7.0**– finish.

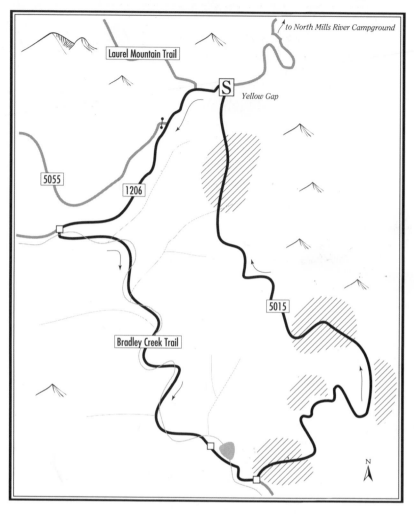

to North Mills River Campground

Laurel Mountain Trail

S

Yellow Gap

5055

1206

5015

Bradley Creek Trail

N

MAP KEY

Bike Route............................

Other Trail or Road...........

Direction of Travel...............

Start/Finish............................. S

Milepost.................................. □

Public Land.....................

Other Land.......................

Recreation/Camping Area... ⛺

Major Mountain..................

River, Lake or Stream.....

Forest Service Rd. #................. 476

Road or Trail Name..... Black Mountain Trail

Foot Travel Only....... ~ ~ ~ ~ ~

Timber Cut or Clearing.. //////

3200'

2480'

Elevation Change

20

Spencer Gap

Taking advantage of gravel roads for most of the climbing, this ride takes you out and up to a ridge just below the Blue Ridge Parkway. You'll return on the fairly technical single track of the Spencer Branch Trail.

Start/Finish

To get to the trailhead, drive north for 2 miles on FS 5000 from North Mills River Campground and then turn left on FS 142 for 0.5 miles.

Trail Configuration

Loop

Surface

Single track • 4.2 miles
Forest road • 3.8 miles

Highlights

Creek crossings, mud bogs, spotty views, short steep climbs, short steep technical downhill, horse use

Total Distance

8.0 miles

Time Allowance

Beginner • 3 hours
Intermediate • 2.25 hours
Advanced • 1.5 hours

Mileposts

- **From start**– ride towards FS 5000 on FS 142.
- **Mile 0.5**– turn left onto FS 5000.
- **Mile 2.6**– turn left onto Spencer Gap Trail. This is marked by a gate on the left in a sharp right bend in the road. The trail sign is 100 feet up the trail **(yellow blaze)**.
- **Mile 2.8**– trail forks just before a field. Take the right fork up the hill and through the field.
- **Mile 4.0**– Spencer Gap. Turn left onto Trace Ridge Trail and then immediately right down Spencer Branch Trail **(yellow blaze)**.
- **Mile 4.8**– cross Fletcher Creek Road.
- **Mile 5.7**– turn left on Fletcher Creek Trail **(blue blaze)**.
- **Mile 6.8**– turn left on Hendersonville Reservoir Road.
- **Mile 8.0**– finish.

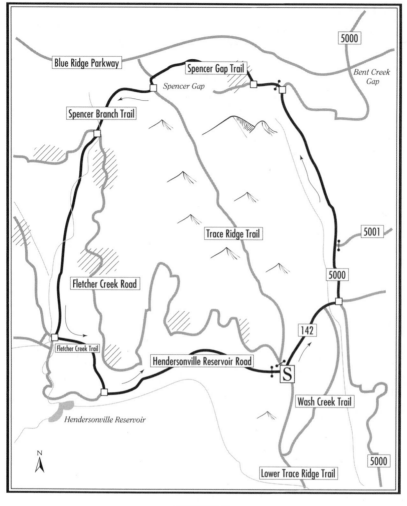

Blue Ridge Parkway

Spencer Gap Trail

Spencer Gap

Bent Creek Gap

5000

Spencer Branch Trail

Trace Ridge Trail

5001

5000

Fletcher Creek Road

142

Fletcher Creek Trail

Hendersonville Reservoir Road

S

Wash Creek Trail

N

Hendersonville Reservoir

5000

Lower Trace Ridge Trail

MAP KEY

Bike Route...........................
Other Trail or Road...........
Direction of Travel...............
Start/Finish...................... S
Milepost..................................... □
Public Land......................
Other Land......................
Recreation/Camping Area... Ⓐ
Major Mountain...................
River, Lake or Stream.....

Forest Service Rd. #................. 476
Road or Trail Name..... Black Mountain Trail
Foot Travel Only.......
Timber Cut or Clearing..

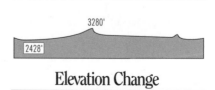

3280'

2428'

Elevation Change

21

Spencer Branch

With relatively few hills, this ride is jazzed up by some rather technical creek crossings and narrow hillside trails. Expect to get muddy on this one, especially after wet weather.

Start/Finish

To get to the trailhead, drive north for 2 miles on FS 5000 from North Mills River Campground and then turn left on FS 142 for 0.5 miles.

Trail Configuration

Loop

Surface

Single track • 6.2 miles
Forest road • 1.9 miles

Highlights

Some technical riding, mud bogs, creek crossings, horse use

Total Distance

8.1 miles

Time Allowance

Beginner • 2 hours
Intermediate • 1.5 hours
Advanced • 1 hour

Mileposts

- **From start**– ride through gate and out Fletcher Creek Road.
- **Mile 4.6**– turn left onto Spencer Branch Trail **(orange blaze)**.
- **Mile 5.5**– cross Fletcher Creek Trail.
- **Mile 5.7**– Middle Fork Trail enters on right. Stay on Spencer Branch Trail.
- **Mile 6.5**– Hendersonville Reservoir. Big Creek Trail enters on right. Spencer Branch Trail ends and Hendersonville Reservoir Road begins. Continue on Hendersonville Reservoir Road.
- **Mile 8.1**– finish.

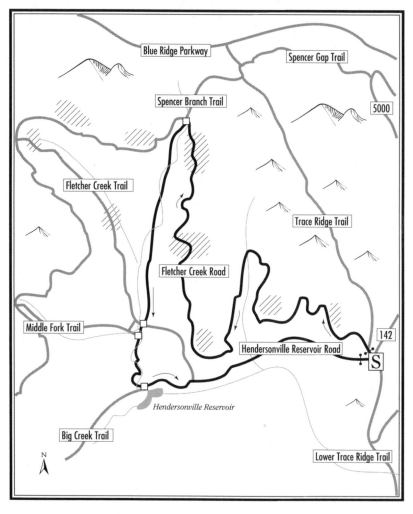

Blue Ridge Parkway

Spencer Gap Trail

Spencer Branch Trail

5000

Fletcher Creek Trail

Trace Ridge Trail

Fletcher Creek Road

Middle Fork Trail

142

Hendersonville Reservoir Road

S

Hendersonville Reservoir

Big Creek Trail

N

Lower Trace Ridge Trail

MAP KEY

Bike Route...........................	
Other Trail or Road...........	
Direction of Travel................	→
Start/Finish.............................	S
Milepost...................................	□
Public Land......................	
Other Land........................	
Recreation/Camping Area...	⛺
Major Mountain...................	
River, Lake or Stream.....	

Forest Service Rd. #.................	476
Road or Trail Name.....	Black Mountain Trail
Foot Travel Only........	- - - - -
Timber Cut or Clearing..	/////

2760'

2560'

Elevation Change

22

Middle Fork

After you take in the views from what is known as the "Never Ending Road," you'll dip down through fern-filled woods, small meadows and alongside a small cascading stream. This one is a real beauty.

Start/Finish

To get to the trailhead, drive north for 2 miles on FS 5000 from North Mills River Campground and then turn left on FS 142 for 0.5 miles.

Trail Configuration

Loop

Surface

Single track • 2.6 miles
Forest road • 9.2 miles

Highlights

Gravel road, views, stream crossings, mud bogs, meadows, open woods, horse use, cascades

Total Distance

11.8 miles

Time Allowance

Beginner • 3 hours
Intermediate • 2 hours
Advanced • 1.25 hours

Mileposts

- **From start**– ride through gate and out Fletcher Creek Road.
- **Mile 4.6**– cross Spencer Branch Trail.
- **Mile 5.6**– Fletcher Creek Trail enters on left.
- **Mile 7.9**– turn left onto Middle Fork Trail **(orange blaze)**.
- **Mile 9.3**– turn right onto Fletcher Creek Trail **(blue blaze)**, cross creek and then cross Spencer Branch Trail.
- **Mile 10.5**– turn left onto Hendersonville Reservoir Road.
- **Mile 11.8**– finish.

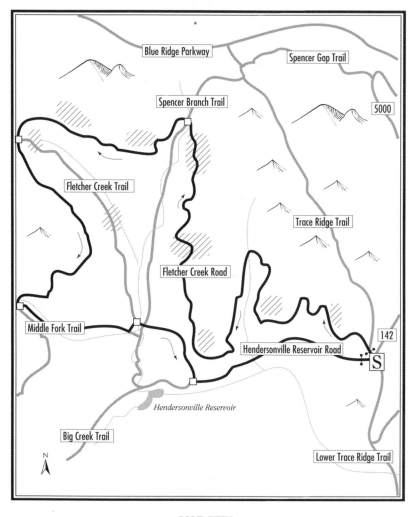

Blue Ridge Parkway

Spencer Gap Trail

5000

Spencer Branch Trail

Fletcher Creek Trail

Trace Ridge Trail

Fletcher Creek Road

Middle Fork Trail

Hendersonville Reservoir Road

142

S

Hendersonville Reservoir

Big Creek Trail

N

Lower Trace Ridge Trail

MAP KEY

Bike Route.......................... 〜

Other Trail or Road........... 〜

Direction of Travel................ →

Start/Finish............................. ⓢ

Milepost.................................. ▫

Public Land.....................

Other Land......................

Recreation/Camping Area... ⛺

Major Mountain..................

River, Lake or Stream.....

Forest Service Rd. #................. 476

Road or Trail Name..... Black Mountain Trail

Foot Travel Only....... ⌁

Timber Cut or Clearing.. ////

2800'

2560'

Elevation Change

MOST DIFFICULT TRAILS

23

Pilot Mountain

High-altitude trails at their best, with spectacular views of John, Cedar and Looking Glass Rocks. There is a hidden turn just past Farlow Gap. You don't want to miss it!

Start/Finish

Gloucester Gap, 5 miles west of Fish Hatchery on FS 475. FS 229, 471 and 475 all meet here.

Trail Configuration

Loop

Surface

Double track • 8.5 miles
Forest road • 2.6 miles

Highlights

Great views, long climbs, very rocky trail sections, whoop-te-doos, cascades, hidden turn

Total Distance

11.1 miles

Time Allowance

Beginner • 4 hours
Intermediate • 3 hours
Advanced • 2 hours

Mileposts

- **From start**– ride up FS 229.
- **Mile 2.6**– road forks, with dirt barriers on each fork. Take the upper (left) fork up the old rocky road bed.
- **Mile 2.8**– Art Loeb/Mountains to Sea Trail enters left.
- **Mile 2.9**– Art Loeb/Mountains to Sea Trail exits left.
- **Mile 4.0**– Farlow Gap. Trails jct. Continue on old road.
- **Mile 4.9**– just after the old washed-out roadbed you are on turns into a newer, seeded road bed, the trail will make two big switchbacks. In the middle of the second one a hidden trail turns off to the left. It's marked by a small dirt barricade. **Turn left here**.
- **Mile 7.5**– unmarked trail enters from the left.
- **Mile 8.0**– 5-way jct. Turn left up gated Indian Creek Road. It's more of a trail than a road.
- **Mile 8.7**– take lower right fork through field.
- **Mile 8.8**– turn left across top of timber cut.
- **Mile 11.1**– finish.

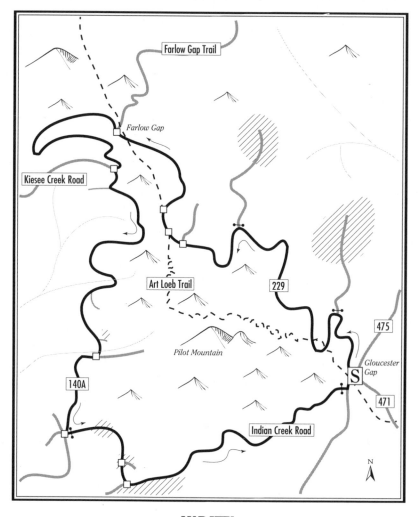

Farlow Gap Trail

Farlow Gap

Kiesee Creek Road

Art Loeb Trail

229

475

Gloucester Gap

Pilot Mountain

140A

S

471

Indian Creek Road

N

MAP KEY

Bike Route............................ 〰

Other Trail or Road........... 〰

Direction of Travel................ →

Start/Finish............................. ⟦S⟧

Milepost................................... □

Public Land......................

Other Land......................

Recreation/Camping Area... ⛺

Major Mountain....................

River, Lake or Stream.....

Forest Service Rd. #.................. ⟦476⟧

Road or Trail Name..... ⟦Black Mountain Trail⟧

Foot Travel Only....... - - - -

Timber Cut or Clearing.. ///////

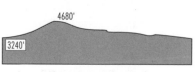

4680'

3240'

Elevation Change

24

Farlow Gap

This is not a ride for someone with bad knees. A long climb is followed by a great ride along the ridge and then a *very* steep downhill that requires a fair amount of carrying.

Start/Finish

Parking pulloff 0.8 miles west of Cove Creek Group Camp on FS 475.

Trail Configuration

Loop

Surface

Single track • 5.6 miles
Forest road • 4.8 miles

Highlights

Great views, 5-mile uphill, *very* steep and rocky downhill, lots of waterfalls

Total Distance

10.4 miles

Time Allowance

Beginner • not recommended
Intermediate • 4.5 hours
Advanced • 3 hours

Mileposts

- **From start**– ride southwest on FS 475.
- **Mile 2.2**– Gloucester Gap. Turn right onto FS 229.
- **Mile 4.8**– road forks, with dirt barricades on each fork. Take the left (upper) fork up rocky old road bed.
- **Mile 5.0**– Art Loeb/Mountains to Sea Trail enters left.
- **Mile 5.1**– Art Loeb/Mountains to Sea Trail exits left.
- **Mile 6.1**– Farlow Gap. Trails jct. here. Turn right onto Farlow Gap Trail **(blue blaze)**.
- **Mile 6.8**– *very* steep downhill to waterfall.
- **Mile 8.6**– turn right on Daniel Ridge Trail **(red blaze)**.
- **Mile 9.0**– old wide log bridge on right. Bear left on Daniel Ridge Trail **(red blaze)**.
- **Mile 9.6**– trail to field bears off to right. Stay left.
- **Mile 10.3**– turn right onto forest road.
- **Mile 10.4**– finish.

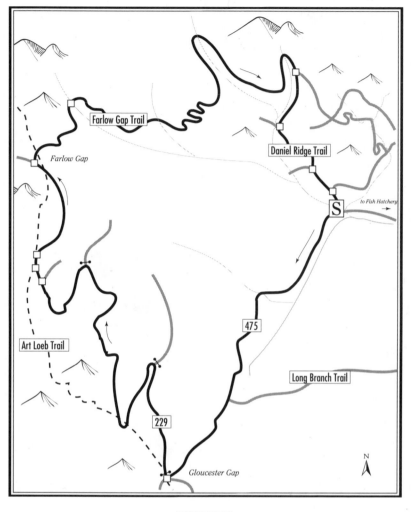

Farlow Gap Trail

Farlow Gap

Daniel Ridge Trail

S

to Fish Hatchery

475

Art Loeb Trail

Long Branch Trail

229

Gloucester Gap

N

MAP KEY

Bike Route............................	～	Forest Service Rd. #.................	476
Other Trail or Road............	～	Road or Trail Name.....	Black Mountain Trail
Direction of Travel...............	→	Foot Travel Only........	– – –
Start/Finish..............................	S	Timber Cut or Clearing..	/////
Milepost....................................	□		
Public Land.........................	▭		
Other Land........................	▬		
Recreation/Camping Area...	▲		
Major Mountain....................	⛰		
River, Lake or Stream.....			

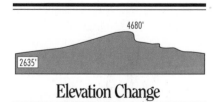

4680'

2635'

Elevation Change

25

Clawhammer

This ride will hammer you. You'll start with a 6-mile climb, the last 1.5 miles of which is a push up steep rock steps. The cliff-top view at the highest point is pretty spectacular— the perfect reward for going the distance.

Start/Finish

Horse stable parking area on FS 477.

Trail Configuration

Loop w/ extension

Surface

Single track • 2.8 miles
Double track • 1.4 miles
Forest road • 6.5 miles

Highlights

Long climb, technical uphill, great views, rock cave, rhododendron tunnel, horse use

Total Distance

10.7 miles

Time Allowance

Beginner • 4 hours
Intermediate • 3 hours
Advanced • 2 hours

Mileposts

- **From start**– ride through gate up Clawhammer Road.
- **Mile 1.0**– Maxwell Cove Road exits to right.
- **Mile 3.8**– unmarked road enters left. Bear right.
- **Mile 4.4**– Buckhorn Gap. 5-way trail junction. Turn right onto Black Mountain/Mountains to Sea Trail **(white blaze w/ white dot)**.
- **Mile 5.6**– spectacular cliff-top view.
- **Mile 6.2**– Turkey Pen Gap Trail **(blue blaze)** enters from left. Stay on Black Mountain Trail **(white blaze)**.
- **Mile 7.2**– Pressley Gap and another 5-way interchange of trails. Take a sharp right down grassy Maxwell Cove Road. Check your speed; there may be horses on their way up.
- **Mile 9.6**– turn left onto Clawhammer Road.
- **Mile 10.7**– finish.

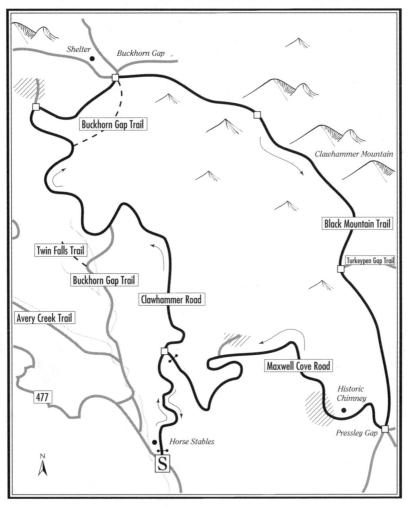

Shelter

Buckhorn Gap

Buckhorn Gap Trail

Clawhammer Mountain

Black Mountain Trail

Twin Falls Trail

Turkeypen Gap Trail

Buckhorn Gap Trail

Clawhammer Road

Avery Creek Trail

Maxwell Cove Road

Historic Chimney

477

Pressley Gap

Horse Stables

N

S

MAP KEY

Bike Route............................ 〰

Other Trail or Road........... 〰

Direction of Travel................. ⟶

Start/Finish............................. S

Milepost.................................. □

Public Land.......................

Other Land........................

Recreation/Camping Area... ⛺

Major Mountain.....................

River, Lake or Stream.....

Forest Service Rd. #................. 476

Road or Trail Name..... Black Mountain Trail

Foot Travel Only....... ⌁

Timber Cut or Clearing.. ///////

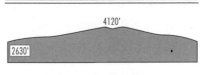

4120'

2630'

Elevation Change

26

Mountains to Mills River

A long mountainous loop, mostly on gravel roads, takes you from the Avery Creek area up and over the ridge to the upper stretches of South Mills River, starting and ending at the Pink Beds.

Start/Finish

Pink Beds Recreation Area on U.S. 276.

Trail Configuration

Loop

Surface

Single track • 3.1 miles
Double track • 0.8 miles
Forest road • 14.8 miles
Pavement • 0.9 miles

Highlights

Views of Looking Glass Rock and other vistas, horse use, long hills, swimming holes, cascades, timber cuts, old rocky road bed

Total Distance

19.6 miles

Time Allowance

Beginner • 5 hours
Intermediate • 3.25 hours
Advanced • 2.5 hours

Mileposts

- **From start**– ride south on U.S. 276 (downhill).
- **Mile 0.5**– turn left onto FS 477.
- **Mile 6.2**– turn left by horse stables up gated Clawhammer Road.
- **Mile 7.2**– Maxwell Cove Road enters from right.
- **Mile 10**– unmarked road enters from left. Bear right.
- **Mile 10.6**– Buckhorn Gap. Black Mountain/Mountains to Sea and Buckhorn Gap trails cross here and the gravel road forks. Take the left fork down the hill. Buckhorn Gap Trail shares this road bed.
- **Mile 11.4**– bear right on Buckhorn Gap Trail **(orange blaze)**.
- **Mile 12.5**– turn left on South Mills River Trail **(white blaze)**.
- **Mile 14.5**– gauging station. Continue on FS 476.
- **Mile 15.9**– Turn left onto FS 1206.
- **Mile 19.2**– turn left onto U.S. 276.
- **Mile 19.6**– finish.

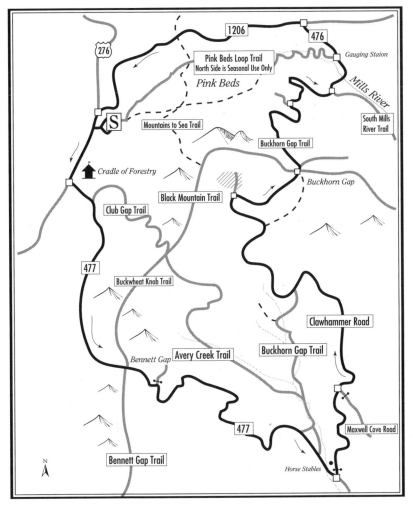

276

1206

476

Gauging Staion

Mills River

Pink Beds Loop Trail
North Side is Seasonal Use Only

Pink Beds

South Mills
River Trail

Mountains to Sea Trail

Buckhorn Gap Trail

🏠 *Cradle of Forestry*

Buckhorn Gap

Black Mountain Trail

Club Gap Trail

477

Buckwheat Knob Trail

Clawhammer Road

Bennett Gap Avery Creek Trail

Buckhorn Gap Trail

477

Maxwell Cove Road

N

Bennett Gap Trail

Horse Stables

MAP KEY

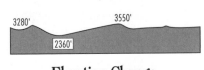

Bike Route........................ 〰

Other Trail or Road........... 〰

Direction of Travel................. →

Start/Finish............................ Ⓢ

Milepost.................................. □

Public Land.....................

Other Land.....................

Recreation/Camping Area... ⛺

Major Mountain...................

River, Lake or Stream.....

Forest Service Rd. #................. 476

Road or Trail Name..... Black Mountain Trail

Foot Travel Only....... - - - -

Timber Cut or Clearing.. ▨

3280'   3550'

2360'

Elevation Change

27

Laurel Mountain

This ride starts out with one of the best single track climbs in Pisgah; all but the last half-mile to the top is pure joy. Well honed technical skills make getting back down a treat in itself. You'll zig and zag through many a rocky switchback before returning to the forest road below.

Start/Finish

Laurel Mountain Trailhead, located 3.5 miles west of North Mills River Campground on FS 1206.

Trail Configuration

Loop

Surface

Single track • 9.1 miles
Forest road • 4.4 miles

Highlights

Gradual climb, rhododendron and laurel tunnels, one very steep uphill pitch, small boulder fields, rocky switchbacks

Total Distance

13.5 miles

Time Allowance

Beginner • 4.5 hours
Intermediate • 3 hours
Advanced • 2 hours

Mileposts

- **From start–** ride uphill on Laurel Mountain Trail **(blue blazes)**.
- **Mile 5.7–** Good Enough Gap. An unmarked trail exits to the right. Bear left to start up a very steep climb.
- **Mile 6.4–** Turkey Spring Gap. Turn left onto Laurel Mountain Connector Trail **(yellow blazes)**.
- **Mile 6.6–** turn left onto Pilot Rock Trail **(orange blazes)**. The next 2.5 miles are all downhill, with technical, rocky switchbacks.
- **Mile 9–** you'll cross an old skid road, a creek and then turn left onto FS 1206.
- **Mile 13.5–** finish.

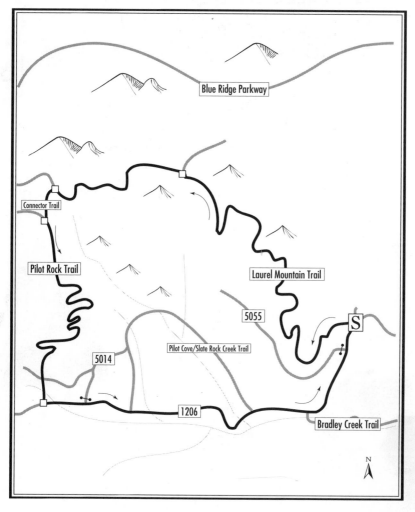

Blue Ridge Parkway

Connector Trail

Pilot Rock Trail

Laurel Mountain Trail

5055

S

Pilot Cove/Slate Rock Creek Trail

5014

1206

Bradley Creek Trail

N

MAP KEY

Bike Route...........................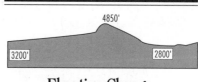

Other Trail or Road...........

Direction of Travel.................

Start/Finish............................. Ⓢ

Milepost.................................. ▫

Public Land......................

Other Land......................

Recreation/Camping Area... ⛺

Major Mountain...................

River, Lake or Stream.....

Forest Service Rd. #................. 476

Road or Trail Name..... Black Mountain Trail

Foot Travel Only.......

Timber Cut or Clearing..

4850'

3200'　　　　　　　　　　2800'

Elevation Change

28

South Mills Tour

This is the longest ride in this book, so allow plenty of time. The multiple stream and river crossings take their toll, but the ride is guaranteed to keep you cool on a hot summer day!

Start/Finish
Bradley Creek Trailhead, 4.8 miles west of North Mills River Campground on FS 1206. It's the first pullout on the left at the bottom of the hill past FS 5015.

Trail Configuration
Loop

Surface
Single track • 18.6 miles
Forest road • 5.3 miles

Highlights
Numerous stream and river crossings, rocky sections, horse use, mud bogs, swinging bridges, few hills, historic lodge site

Total Distance
23.9 miles

Time Allowance
Beginner • 7 hours
Intermediate • 5 hours
Advanced • 4 hours

Mileposts

- **From start**– cross creek and ride downstream on the Bradley Creek Trail **(orange blazes)**.
- **Mile 1.9**– FS 5015 enters left then Laurel Creek Trail right.
- **Mile 2.2**– at end of last big field, cross creek to right.
- **Mile 3.1**– take right fork and begin heading uphill.
- **Mile 3.7**– Squirrel Gap Trail enters on right. Bear left.
- **Mile 4.3**– Riverside Trail enters from left. Bear right.
- **Mile 5.1**– 4-way trails jct. Turn right and cross river on South Mills River Trail **(white blazes)**. You'll follow this trail the next 13.5 miles with many river crossings.
- **Mile 13.9**– Squirrel Gap Trail enters on right. Cross bridge. A little ways farther the trail turns sharply back to the left. Continue to follow the **white blazes**.
- **Mile 18.6**– trail ends and FS 476 begins.
- **Mile 20.0**– turn right onto FS 1206.
- **Mile 23.9**– finish.

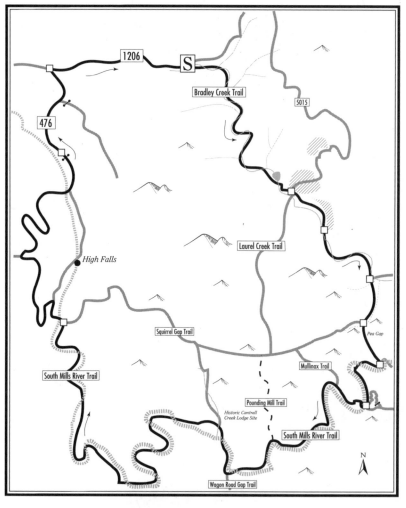

S

Bradley Creek Trail

5015

476

High Falls

Laurel Creek Trail

Squirrel Gap Trail

Pea Gap

South Mills River Trail

Mullinax Trail

Pounding Mill Trail

Historic Cantrell
Creek Lodge Site

South Mills River Trail

Wagon Road Gap Trail

N

MAP KEY

Bike Route.........................	∿
Other Trail or Road...........	∿
Direction of Travel................	→
Start/Finish...........................	S
Milepost..............................	□
Public Land.......................	
Other Land........................	
Recreation/Camping Area...	⛺
Major Mountain..................	
River, Lake or Stream......	

Forest Service Rd. #.................	476
Road or Trail Name.....	Black Mountain Trail
Foot Travel Only........	- - - - -
Timber Cut or Clearing..	/////

3360'

2740'

Elevation Change

Trace Ridge

The most difficult trail (although not extremely so) in the popular Fletcher Creek area. You'll climb steadily and sometimes steeply for most of the first two miles before dropping quite quickly down to Fletcher Creek Road for the return.

Start/Finish

To get to the trailhead, drive north for 2 miles on FS 5000 from North Mills River Campground and then turn left onto FS 140 for 0.5 miles.

Trail Configuration

Loop

Surface

Single track • 2.8 miles
Forest road • 4.6 miles

Highlights

Long rocky climb, ridge riding, spotty views, timber cuts, steep downhill, horse use

Total Distance

7.4 miles

Time Allowance

Beginner • 2.5 hours
Intermediate • 1.75 hours
Advanced • 1 hour

Mileposts

- **From start–** ride through gate onto Fletcher Creek Road and then immediately take a right up over whoop-te-doos onto Trace Ridge Trail **(orange blazes)**.
- Mile 1.7– top of ridge.
- Mile 2.0– turn left down Spencer Branch Trail **(yellow blazes)**. This is *very* steep.
- Mile 2.8– turn left onto Fletcher Creek Road. This is known locally as the **"Never Ending Road."**
- Mile 7.4– finish.

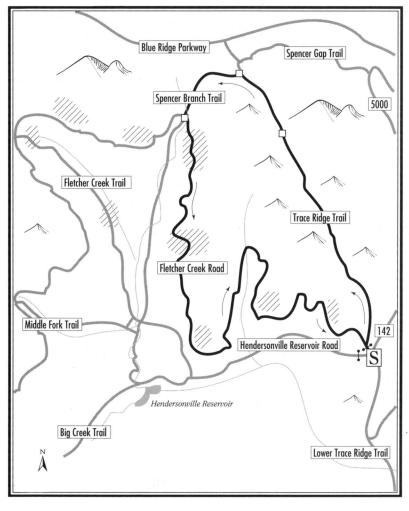

MAP KEY

Bike Route............................	～	Forest Service Rd. #.................	476
Other Trail or Road...........	～	Road or Trail Name.....	Black Mountain Trail
Direction of Travel...............	→	Foot Travel Only........	- - - - -
Start/Finish............................	S	Timber Cut or Clearing..	//////
Milepost..................................	□		
Public Land......................	▭		
Other Land.......................	▨		
Recreation/Camping Area...	⛺		
Major Mountain..................	⛰		
River, Lake or Stream.....			

Elevation Change

3480'
2560'

SEASONAL TRAILS

Forest Service regulations permit use of these trails by mountain bikers from October 15 to April 15 only.

30

North Slope

With its short but steep hills, this trail is great by itself or it can be a nice addition to any of the rides leaving from the district ranger station.

Start/Finish
Art Loeb Trailhead parking lot just off U.S. 276 at entrance to Davidson River Campground.

Trail Configuration
Loop w/ extension

Surface
Single track • 4 miles
Pavement • 0.3 miles

Highlights
Spotty views, Davidson River, short steep uphill, ridge ride, rhododendron tunnels, mud bog

Total Distance
4.3 miles

Time Allowance
Beginner • 1.5 hours
Intermediate • 1 hour
Advanced • 40 minutes

Mileposts

- **From start**– ride across Davidson River, past the Exercise Trail and into Davidson River Campground.
- **Mile 0.3**– Pass the amphitheater parking area and start the loop. Continue through the campground to the last bath house.
- **Mile 1.4**– turn left onto the North Slope Trail. Follow the **orange blazes** along the river past the cemetery and then take a sharp left up the hill.
- **Mile 2.1**– North Slope Connector Trail enters from right. Stay to left on North Slope Trail.
- **Mile 3.9**– almost back to campground. Several trails go in all directions. Watch for **orange blazes**.
- **Mile 4.0**– Amphitheater parking area. Turn right and head out of campground.
- **Mile 4.3**– finish.

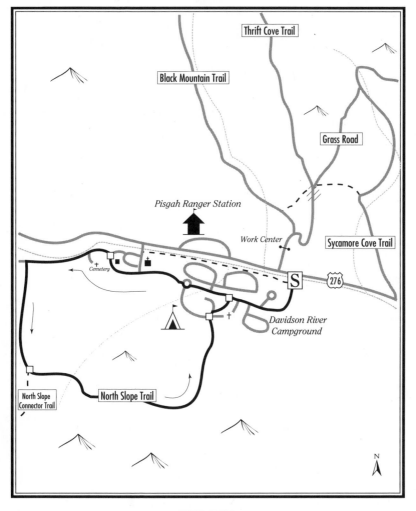

MAP KEY

Bike Route..........................	~
Other Trail or Road...........	~
Direction of Travel..............	→
Start/Finish............................	S
Milepost.................................	□
Public Land......................	▭
Other Land.......................	▬
Recreation/Camping Area...	🏕
Major Mountain..................	🏔
River, Lake or Stream.....	〰

Forest Service Rd. #.................	476
Road or Trail Name.....	Black Mountain Trail
Foot Travel Only........	- - -
Timber Cut or Clearing..	/////

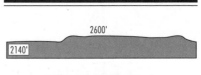

2600'

2140'

Elevation Change

31

Butter Gap

After a long climb on forest roads you'll find a wide trail up to Butter Gap and the foot of Cedar Rock's cliffs. Check your brake cables because the last 3.5 miles are all downhill.

Start/Finish
State Fish Hatchery on FS 475.

Trail Configuration
Loop

Surface
Single track • 4.3 miles
Forest road • 7.5 miles

Highlights
Spotty views, Cedar Rock, waterfall, technical sections

Total Distance
11.8 miles

Time Allowance
Beginner • 4 hours
Intermediate • 2.5 hours
Advanced • 1.75 hours

Mileposts

- **From start**– cross bridge and turn left onto FS 475.
- **Mile 4.8**– Gloucester Gap. Turn left onto FS 471.
- **Mile 7**– Turn left onto unmarked gated road. This is the second gated road on the left after crossing the Art Loeb Trail. It quickly becomes a trail.
- **Mile 7.5**– bear right at trail fork past old gate.
- **Mile 7.8**– 5-way jct. of trails. Cross Art Loeb and head around north side of ridge.
- **Mile 8**– Butter Gap. 7-way jct. of trails. There's a side hike here up Cedar Rock. Turn sharply to left downhill on Butter Gap Trail (**blue blaze**).
- **Mile 10.2**– Long Branch Trail enters left. Bear right.
- **Mile 10.7**– pass through Picklesimer Fields and turn left onto Cat Gap Trail (**orange blaze**).
- **Mile 11**– bear right at trail fork.
- **Mile 11.3**– turn left on forest road back to hatchery.
- **Mile 11.8**– finish.

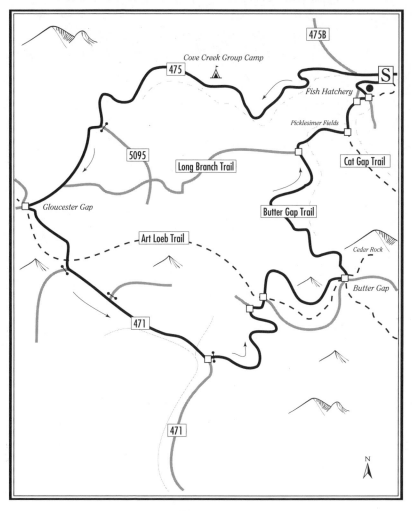

MAP KEY

Bike Route............................	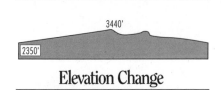	Forest Service Rd. #.................	476
Other Trail or Road...........		Road or Trail Name.....	Black Mountain Trail
Direction of Travel................	→	Foot Travel Only.......	- - - -
Start/Finish............................	S	Timber Cut or Clearing..	/////
Milepost...................................	□		
Public Land........................	▭		
Other Land........................	▬		
Recreation/Camping Area...	⛺		
Major Mountain..................			
River, Lake or Stream.....			

Elevation Change

3440'

2350'

32

Picklesimer Fields

With equal amounts of single track and gravel roads, this is quite the ride. You'll enjoy testing your skills on the log bridges and rutted hills while taking in views of John Rock, several waterfalls and, of course, Picklesimer Fields.

Start/Finish
State Fish Hatchery on FS 475.

Trail Configuration
Loop

Surface
Single track • 4.2 miles
Forest road • 4.2 miles

Highlights
Long uphill on gravel road, rhododendron tunnels, rutted trail, log bridges, rock slabs, waterfalls and cascades, views

Total Distance
8.4 miles

Time Allowance
Beginner • 2.5 hours
Intermediate • 2 hours
Advanced • 1.25 hours

Mileposts

- **From start**– cross bridge and turn left onto FS 475.
- **Mile 3.1**– gated FS 5095 on left. Continue on FS 475.
- **Mile 4.2**– Cemetery Loop Trail enters on left. Continue 100 yds. farther and turn left onto Long Branch Trail **(orange blaze)**.
- **Mile 5.0**– jct. Cemetery Loop Trail. Stay right on Long Branch Trail.
- **Mile 6.0**– cross logging road.
- **Mile 6.9**– turn left on Butter Gap Trail **(blue blaze)**.
- **Mile 7.4**– Picklesimer Fields.
- **Mile 7.5**– turn left on Cat Gap Trail **(orange blaze)**.
- **Mile 8.0**– cross gravel road and then a foot bridge.
- **Mile 8.4**– finish.

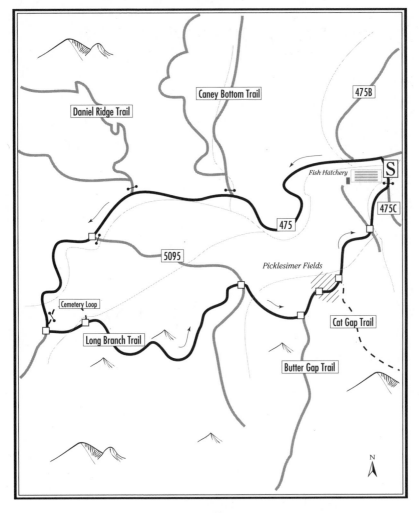

MAP KEY

Bike Route..........................		Forest Service Rd. #.................	476
Other Trail or Road...........		Road or Trail Name.....	Black Mountain Trail
Direction of Travel...............	→	Foot Travel Only.......	- - - -
Start/Finish............................	S	Timber Cut or Clearing..	///
Milepost..................................	□		
Public Land......................			
Other Land......................			
Recreation/Camping Area...	⛺		
Major Mountain..................			
River, Lake or Stream.....			

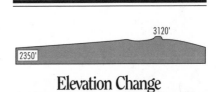

3120'

2350'

Elevation Change

33

Bennett Gap

After a grunt of a climb you'll find a trail that snakes along the top of a knife-like ridge with cliff-top views of Looking Glass Rock and Clawhammer Mountain. Short sections are so technical it seems as if your wheels will barely hang on. The ride to the bottom is a hoot.

Start/Finish
Horse stable parking on FS 477.

Trail Configuration
Loop

Surface
Single track • 2.9 miles
Forest road • 3.6 miles

Highlights
Long climb, technical rocky sections, views

Total Distance
6.5 miles

Time Allowance
Beginner • 3 hours
Intermediate • 1.75 hours
Advanced • 1 hour

Mileposts

- **From start**– ride uphill on FS 477.
- **Mile 3.2**– Bennett Gap. Turn left onto Bennett Gap Trail **(red blaze)**.
- **Mile 3.8**– cliff-top view of Looking Glass Rock.
- **Mile 4.5**– Coontree Loop Trail enters from right and shares this trail.
- **Mile 5.1**– Coontree Loop Trail exits to right. Stay left.
- **Mile 6.1**– turn left onto FS 477.
- **Mile 6.5**– finish.

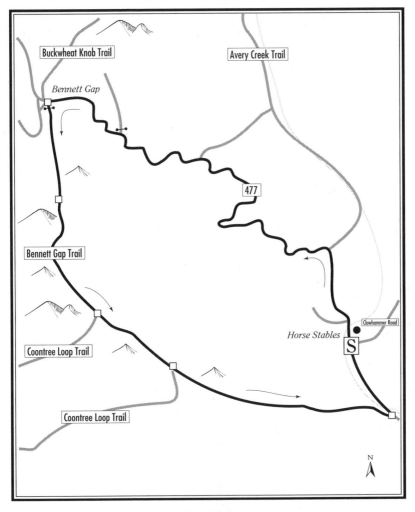

Buckwheat Knob Trail

Avery Creek Trail

Bennett Gap

477

Bennett Gap Trail

Coontree Loop Trail

Coontree Loop Trail

Horse Stables

Clawhammer Road

S

N

MAP KEY

Bike Route............................ 〰

Forest Service Rd. #................. 476

Other Trail or Road............ 〰

Road or Trail Name..... Black Mountain Trail

Direction of Travel............... →

Foot Travel Only....... - - - - -

Start/Finish............................ S

Timber Cut or Clearing.. ▨

Milepost.................................. □

Public Land........................ ▭

Other Land........................ ▭

Recreation/Camping Area... ⛺

Major Mountain...................

River, Lake or Stream.....

3494'

2360'

Elevation Change

34

The Pink Beds

This relatively flat area gets its name from the abundance of pink flowering plants. You won't see many flowers during the winter months, but you will enjoy the gently rolling terrain.

Start/Finish

Pink Beds parking area on U.S. 276.

Trail Configuration

Loop

Surface

Single track • 4.8 miles
Forest road • 3.3 miles
Pavement • 0.4 miles

Highlights

Views from meadows, rhododendron tunnels, log bridges, rooty trail, South Mills River, interpretive signs

Total Distance

8.5 miles

Time Allowance

Beginner • 2.25 hours
Intermediate • 1.5 hours
Advanced • 1 hour

Mileposts

- **From start**– ride through gate onto Pink Beds Loop Trail **(orange blaze)**.
- **Mile 0.1**– take left fork of loop trail. The right fork is closed to bikes.
- **Mile 1.0**– cross Mountains to Sea Trail (marked by round white dot).
- **Mile 2.5**– turn left at trail jct. and look for **white blazes**. This is the Pink Beds Loop Extension. You'll be heading downstream beside the upper South Mills River.
- **Mile 3.4**– gauging station. Turn left onto FS 476.
- **Mile 4.8**– turn left onto FS 1206.
- **Mile 8.1**– turn left onto U.S. 276.
- **Mile 8.5**– finish.

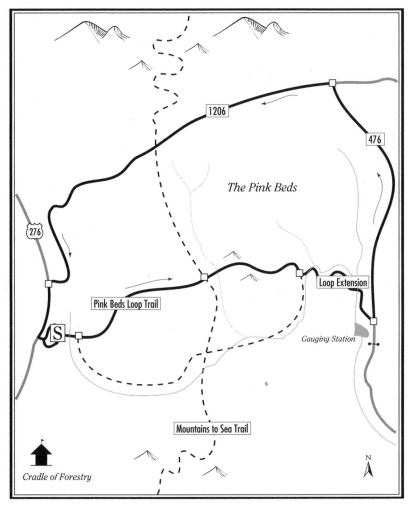

The Pink Beds

1206

476

276

Loop Extension

Pink Beds Loop Trail

Gauging Station

S

Mountains to Sea Trail

N

Cradle of Forestry

MAP KEY

Bike Route...................... ⌇	Forest Service Rd. #.................. 476
Other Trail or Road........... ⌇	Road or Trail Name..... Black Mountain Trail
Direction of Travel................ →	Foot Travel Only....... - - - -
Start/Finish............................. S	Timber Cut or Clearing.. /////
Milepost............................. □	
Public Land...................... ▭	
Other Land...................... ▬	
Recreation/Camping Area... ⛺	
Major Mountain.................. ⛰	
River, Lake or Stream.....	

3280'

3150'

Elevation Change

Regional Information

Local Bike Resources
Lodging & Camping
Weather

Local Bike Resources

Asheville Area

- **Liberty Bicycles**
  1987 Hendersonville Hwy.
  Asheville, NC 28803
  704/684-1085
  Sales, rentals and repair services.

- **Pro Bikes of Asheville**
  342 Merrimon Ave.
  Asheville, NC 28801
  704/253-2800
  Sales and repair services.

- **Carolina Fatz Mountain Bike Center**
  1500 Brevard Road
  Asheville, NC 28806
  704/298-2292
  Sales, rentals and repair services.

- **J. M. Hearn Cycleworks**
  34 Broadway
  Asheville, NC 28801
  704/253-4800
  Sales and repair services.

- **Black Mountain Bicycles**
  108 Black Mountain Ave.
  Black Mountain, NC 28711
  704/669-5969
  Sales and repair services.

Brevard/Hendersonville Area

- **Bikeways**
  607 Greenville Hwy.
  Hendersonville, NC 28739
  704/692-0613
  Sales and repair services.

- **Pisgah Bike Center**
  210 East Main Street
  Brevard, NC 28712
  704/966-9606
  Sales and repair services.

- **Backcountry Outfitters**
  P.O. Box 1450
  Highways 276, 64 & 280
  Pisgah Forest, NC 28768
  704/833-9453
  Sales, rentals and repair services.

Lodging & Camping

- **Key Falls Inn**
  151 Everett Road
  Pisgah Forest, NC 28768
  704/884-7559
  Bed & Breakfast, away from town, close to most trails, reasonable prices.

- **The Pisgah Inn**
  P.O. Drawer 749
  Waynesville, NC 28786
  704/235-8228
  Located on the Blue Ridge Parkway, great views, restaurant, open April – November.

For a complete listing contact: Brevard Chamber of Commerce
35 W. Main Street
Brevard, NC 28712
704/883-3700

National Forest Campgrounds

- **Davidson River Campground**
  First-come, first-served; designated sites; per-site fee; hot showers; closed in winter.

- **North Mills River Campground**
  First-come, first-served; designated sites; per-site fee; hot showers; closed in winter.

- **Cove Creek Group Camp**
  Reservations required, groups only, primitive facilities.

- **White Pines Group Camp**
  Reservations required, groups only, primitive facilities.

For more information contact: Pisgah Ranger District
1001 Pisgah Hwy.
Pisgah Forest, NC 28768
704/877-3265

In the Pisgah District, free roadside camping is permitted in areas so designated by a sign. Camping is also permitted anywhere in the backcountry if you are at least 500 feet from an open road.

Weather

Month	Average Temperature*		Average Rainfall
	High	Low	(in inches)
January	47.5°	26°	3.48"
February	50.6°	27.6°	3.6"
March	58.4°	34.4°	5.13"
April	68.6°	42.7°	3.84"
May	75.6°	51°	4.19"
June	81.4°	58.2°	4.2"
July	84°	62.4°	4.43"
August	83.5°	61.6°	4.79"
September	77.9°	55.8°	3.96"
October	68.7°	43.3°	3.29"
November	58.6°	34.2°	3.29"
December	50.3°	28.2°	3.51"

*All temperatures are Fahrenheit. Information provided by the National Weather Service.